WOMEN WIN THE VOTE!

▮▮▮▮▮▮▮▮▮▮▮▮▮▮▮▮▮▮▮▮▮▮▮▮▮

19 FOR THE
19TH AMENDMENT

Nancy B. Kennedy

Illustrated by Katy Dockrill

Norton Young Readers

An Imprint of W. W. Norton & Company
Independent Publishers Since 1923

For information about permission to reproduce selections from this book, write to
Permissions, W. W. Norton & Company, Inc., 500 Fifth Avenue, New York, NY 10110

For information about special discounts for bulk purchases, please contact
W. W. Norton Special Sales at specialsales@wwnorton.com or 800-233-4830

Manufacturing by Versa
Book design by Kristine Noel Brogno
Production manager: Anna Oler

ISBN 978-1-324-00414-1

W. W. Norton & Company, Inc.
500 Fifth Avenue, New York, N.Y. 10110
www.wwnorton.com

W. W. Norton & Company Ltd.
15 Carlisle Street, London W1D 3BS

1 2 3 4 5 6 7 8 9 0

For my own suffragents, John and Evan

Acknowledgments

I have Joëlle Delbourgo to thank for fully embracing my idea and for handing me over to her colleague, my fabulous agent, Jacquie Flynn. The very moment Simon Boughton shared his vision for the book, I was hooked, and illustrator Katy Dockrill brought it to vivid life. Thank you to Simon and to Kristin Allard, and the entire team at Norton Young Readers, for celebrating the woman's suffrage fight with me.

THE NINETEENTH AMENDMENT

1. The right of citizens of the United States to vote shall not be denied or abridged by the United States or by any State on account of sex.

2. Congress shall have power to enforce this article by appropriate legislation.

Contents

Introduction

WHERE DID WOMEN'S RIGHT TO VOTE COME FROM?

THE RIGHT TO VOTE—we hardly give it a thought these days. Once we've turned eighteen, we can register as voters, and then, on Election Day, we head to our local polling place to cast our ballot. We elect school board members, sheriffs, lawmakers, presidents, sometimes even judges. This right is known as suffrage.

This simple act of citizenship hasn't always been the right of all Americans. Far from it. For most of our nation's history, only men—and only white men, at that— could vote. The Constitution of the United States, the document that became our country's governing law in 1789, spoke of "persons" and not "men." But in practice, and later through laws and court rulings, women were excluded.

Most men—and some women—believed women just didn't have what it takes to vote.

At first, only free white men over the age of twenty-one who were educated and owned property could vote in our country. These limits left out a huge swath of people—in the first presidential election held in 1789, only 6 percent of the population had the right to vote.

This division between who could and could not vote became unbearable for those who were denied the franchise. Eventually, women decided they'd had enough and began to push back. Local groups started gathering, and in 1848, the first large-scale gathering devoted to women's rights in the United States took place in Seneca Falls, New York.

These fearless females got the ball rolling!

Our form of democracy allows the Constitution to be changed, or amended. After the Seneca Falls convention, women began to fight for an amendment that would grant them the right to vote. Their single-minded purpose earned them the title of suffragist. They traveled across the country speaking to puzzled audiences who had never heard women speak in public. They lobbied lawmakers who had never faced women determined to have their way.

Finally, in 1878, suffragists succeeded in having their amendment introduced in Congress. But congressmen weren't interested. They were afraid women would vote for people and issues they didn't agree with. Year after year, the amendment was introduced, but it wasn't acted on until 1887, when the Senate voted on and defeated the amendment. Despite the setback, suffragists continued to have the amendment introduced every year.

As the years passed, the suffrage campaign lost steam. During the Civil War—and later World War I—the nation's attention was focused on the war effort. Suffrage groups split over the issue of voting rights for African Americans. Some women worked to gain the vote state by state, while others insisted an amendment to the Constitution was the only solution. Suffragists became divided even by tactics—some lost patience with polite lobbying and became militant. If they landed in jail? So much the better! Anything to bring attention to the cause.

When the amendment reached Congress in 1919, forty-one years after the suffragists' first attempt, lawmakers were finally listening, and this time it passed. But in order to become law, it needed the approval of thirty-six states. Suffragists began an intense state-by-state battle. Their hard work paid off—on August 18, 1920, the Nineteenth Amendment was ratified. Now it was illegal for states or the federal government to deny citizens the right to vote because of their gender. In the presidential election that year, an estimated 10 million women voted for the first time.

In this book, you'll meet nineteen women who paved the way for the vote. Among them are Lucretia Mott, a Quaker who became the mother of the women's rights movement, and Sojourner Truth, a former slave who knew the plight of the oppressed all too well. You'll meet Susan B. Anthony, who was jailed for voting, and Abby Kelley Foster, who refused to pay taxes to an all-male government. Also leading the campaign were Ida B. Wells-Barnett, an African American journalist who refused to walk in a segregated section of a suffrage march; Adelina Otero-Warren, an Hispano woman who led the suffrage fight in New Mexico; and Jeannette Rankin, the first woman elected to Congress.

Millions devoted their lives to this fight— they marched, they protested, they held conventions and gave speeches, they lobbied, wrote articles, and drew cartoons. They were bullied and mocked as man-haters, monsters, and traitors to their sex. They became outcasts in their homes and in their communities. For their actions, they were thrown into filthy, freezing prison cells, where they were beaten and shackled to their cell doors and fed worm-ridden slop. They went on hunger strikes and were held down while prison doctors thrust feeding tubes down their throats. Their resolve was tested daily.

One hundred years ago, women won a hard-fought civil rights victory. For 144 years, our country denied women the vote—seventy-two years passed from our nation's founding in 1776 until the first stirrings of the suffrage movement in Seneca Falls. For another seventy-two years, women fought valiantly. Theirs was a cause that cost many women their reputations, their families and friends, their health, and, for some, even their lives.

It's something to consider while you stand in line at the polls with your parents—and when eventually you cast your own vote.

QUAKERism does not mean quietism.

Lucretia Coffin Mott

JANUARY 3, 1793–NOVEMBER 11, 1880

I AM NO ADVOCATE OF PASSIVITY.

LUCRETIA COFFIN was never afraid to break the rules. One day at boarding school, a boy was locked in a closet without his dinner for misbehaving. Eleven-year-old Lucretia and a friend sneaked through hallways and stairwells to the boys' side of the school, where they slipped bread and butter under the door for him. They got back without being caught!

Lucretia grew up on the island of Nantucket, off the coast of Massachusetts. Her father was a ship captain who was away from home often, leaving her mother in charge of the family store. When her mother traveled to Boston to buy goods for the store, Lucretia managed the house and cared for her brothers and sisters.

The Motts were a Quaker family. Quakers believe that everyone has a divine inner spirit and that anyone who feels the leading of this spirit can speak in church. Because of this belief, Lucretia was used to hearing women speak boldly. As an adult, Lucretia became a traveling Quaker speaker herself.

In the early 1800s, Lucretia taught at a school in Millbrook, New York, where she had been a student. She saw that girls weren't getting the same education boys were, and that female teachers were paid less than males. "I resolved to claim for myself all that an impartial Creator had bestowed," she said.

Lucretia began to speak out against slavery, believing it should be abolished immediately. Not everyone agreed. Some thought the church should stay out of it, while others believed it should happen more slowly. Some even thought slaves should be sent away to another country. But Lucretia stood firm. "If our principles are right, why should we be cowards?" she said.

In 1840, Lucretia went to London with her husband, James Mott, for the World Anti-Slavery Convention. But the male delegates didn't want female delegates there. For an entire day the women listened to men argue about whether they could participate. "The discussion grew more bitter, personal, and exasperating every hour," one woman noted. Finally, the men voted that women couldn't speak and had to sit behind a curtained rail.

Lucretia received more education than most girls of her time. Quakers believed in treating boys and girls the same. Still, by age fifteen, she had finished school and become a teacher.

Outraged, Lucretia and the other women built a fire in the central hearth of their hotel and kept it burning through the night. In the middle of June! Disgusted—and no doubt sweating up a storm—some of the men fled the hotel.

That day, Lucretia saw that women were being denied a role in public life. She realized that men had to stop telling women what they could and couldn't do. Laws and traditions would not change until women had a voice.

At the convention, Lucretia met Elizabeth Cady Stanton, a young newlywed who shared her outrage. In 1848, they met again at a friend's house in Seneca Falls, a small town in central New York State. There, a group of five women discussed the ways men controlled women's lives. They decided to hold a two-day meeting at the town's Wesleyan Methodist chapel. They placed an ad in the local paper for "a Convention to discuss the social, civil and religious condition and rights of woman."

On July 19, 1848, more than three hundred people showed up. Streets were clogged with horses, wagons, and people. Even some men wanted to attend. Did the women bar the doors? No! They didn't treat men the way women had been treated in London.

At the convention, the organizers presented a paper patterned after the Declaration of Independence called the Declaration of Sentiments and Resolutions. "We hold these truths to be self-evident: that all men and women are created equal," it began. In a long list of societal ills and action points, the document described how men oppressed women and how women intended to change things. It introduced the idea of women's equality with men and a woman's claim to all the rights of an American citizen.

Oddly enough, a demand for the woman's vote was hotly debated. Some people— even Lucretia—believed that focusing on the vote alone would take attention away from other issues, such as property rights and access to education. Others even believed that women weren't smart enough to vote or that they could simply convince men to vote for their causes.

Dressed in her black and white Quaker dress and bonnet, Lucretia was a motherly figure who put everyone at ease, even when her ideas sounded radical. Her speech was peppered with quaint "thee's" and "thou's" in the Quaker way, making hers a calming voice in a time of rising unrest.

Quakers were pacifists who believed they shouldn't take part in a government that could declare and engage in war, even by voting. But Lucretia didn't consider civil rights battles as wars to shrink from. "I am no advocate of passivity," she said. "Quakerism, as I understand it, does not mean quietism." Today, Lucretia Mott is considered a founder of the American women's rights movement.

In the United States

in the early 1800s, women couldn't vote, serve on a jury, or be a witness in court. Girls were rarely educated beyond elementary school, and, until 1837, not a single college that admitted men would admit women. If they worked, women generally were teachers or held menial jobs. Most people believed a woman should stay at home, caring for her husband and children.

A married woman was the property of her husband. She could not own land, sign contracts, or keep her earnings, even if she just sold eggs or butter. She didn't even own her own clothes! If her husband was violent, an alcoholic, or gambled away their home, the law wouldn't step in. Only a man could divorce, and the husband got sole custody of any children.

Our nation's Constitution wasn't clear on exactly who could vote. In fact, New Jersey's constitution, written in 1776, allowed some unmarried women to vote, but that right was taken away in 1807. From then on, voting in this country was considered a man's right, especially after the Fourteenth Amendment entered the word "male" into the Constitution in 1868, giving voting rights only to men.

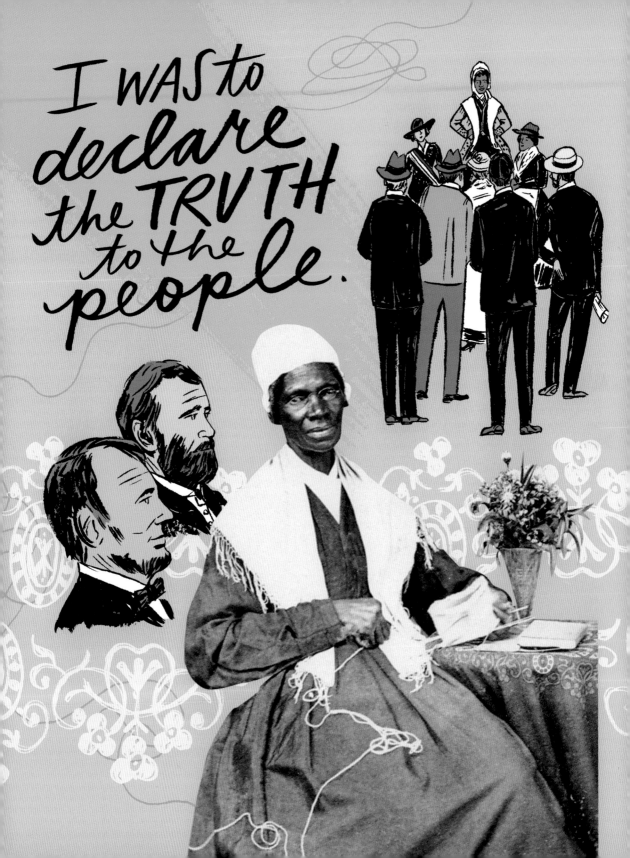

I WAS to declare the TRUTH to the people.

2

Sojourner Truth

C. 1797–NOVEMBER 26, 1883

YOU MAY HISS AS MUCH AS YOU PLEASE, BUT WOMEN WILL GET THEIR RIGHTS ANYWAY.

IT'S HARD TO IMAGINE being able to change the way people think or act if you can't read or write, or even sign your name. But one woman who was entirely illiterate made her mark on the world anyway. Her name was Sojourner Truth.

Born into slavery in New Paltz, New York, Sojourner was often beaten as a child— once with heated iron rods because she didn't understand English, only the Dutch she had learned from her first owner. One of her owners housed his slaves in a damp, un-heated, dirt-floor basement that regularly flooded. Sojourner once saw a slave killed with a blow to the head. "Oh! my God! What a way is this of treating human beings?" she cried.

Enslaved children weren't educated, but Sojourner's parents passed down stories from their family history and the Bible. Sojourner fully embraced this way of learn-ing—as a suffrage and an antislavery activist, she made a lasting impression through her own stories, poems, and songs.

New York State began freeing slaves at the end of the 1700s. Sojourner's owner promised to free her in 1826, when she was about thirty years old, but he didn't. "Ah! The slaveholders are terrible for promising to give you this or that . . . and when the time of fulfillment comes . . . they recollect nothing of the kind: and you are . . . taunted

Sojourner Truth's

name was a powerful symbol of her life's work. But it was not the name she was given at birth.

Sojourner was named Isabelle at birth, and she was called Belle. Her parents went by Baumfree and Mau Mau Bett. Slaves did not have last names—they were given the last name of the slave owner. Belle's last name was changed for each of the owners she had before she escaped—Hardenbergh for two owners, then Neely, Schryver, and Dumont.

As a freewoman, Belle didn't want a name that had defined her as a slave. She wanted to be known as a reformer, a person who works to change society for the better. In 1843, when she started speaking out against slavery, she chose the name Sojourner, meaning a person who doesn't stay in one place. To her, that name described her God-given mission as a traveling speaker for reform causes. Wanting a last name to call her own, she chose Truth because, she said, "I was to declare the truth to the people."

with being a liar," she said. She escaped one morning that year, taking only her baby and leaving her other four children with their father.

A Quaker family took Sojourner in when she first escaped. Many Quakers helped escaped slaves on their own or through the Underground Railroad, a route of safe houses leading north. Sojourner moved from place to place, living where she had friends or could find work.

In the mid-1840s, Sojourner began speaking out against slavery. She criss-crossed the country, speaking to audiences that included both men and women. In those days, women didn't speak in public at all, let alone to audiences of both sexes. Not only that, but Sojourner most often spoke to white audiences. An African American woman telling white people what to do? And a former slave at that! Sojourner was a bold woman who claimed her space in the free world.

At over six feet tall, Sojourner towered over people, and her piercing stare and confident voice made her someone who couldn't be ignored. But she didn't bully people. In 1852, at a meeting in Akron, Ohio, she walked up the aisle of a church and sat down quietly on the steps to the pulpit. She didn't say a word while other people spoke. But when she was ready, she asked for permission to speak.

Sojourner could see that women were being denied their rights, just as slaves were. She began to speak out for suffrage. "Man is in a tight place, the poor slave is on him, woman is coming on him, he is surely between a hawk and a buzzard," she declared.

Often, she called on her audience's background of faith to make her points. "I have heard the Bible and have learned that Eve caused man to sin," she would say. "Well, if woman upset the world, do give her a chance to set it right side up again."

Sojourner didn't shy away from scolding anyone who heckled her. "You may hiss as much as you please, but women will get their rights anyway," she once told an audience of angry men who were booing her speech.

Her lack of education held Sojourner back in some ways. People had to write letters for her and organize her speaking schedule. She needed help reading train schedules, newspaper articles, and documents. Often, a grandson would serve as her aide. But she was widely respected and was even invited to meet with presidents Abraham Lincoln and Ulysses S. Grant.

Sojourner Truth was the first African American woman to win a court case against a white person in the United States. In 1828, she sued a slave owner who had illegally sold her five-year-old son and won his freedom.

Although she never took a leadership role, Sojourner worked closely with Lucretia Mott and the early suffrage movement's other leaders. She backed the cause for decades, speaking publicly well into her eighties. She was a powerful advocate for the cause, convincing people not with academic argument, but with fiery homespun talk that stirred her listeners' emotions.

3

Abby Kelley Foster

JANUARY 15, 1811–JANUARY 14, 1887

BLOODY FEET, SISTERS, HAVE WORN SMOOTH THE PATH BY WHICH YOU COME UP HITHER.

ABBY KELLEY once walked into a church service in Connecticut and, at the sight of her, the preacher shouted out a warning to his congregation.

"This Jezebel is come among us also!" he cried, likening her to a biblical villain of low reputation.

What had this young woman done to deserve such public scorn?

Born into a middle-class Quaker farm family in Pelham, Massachusetts, Abby was educated to become a teacher. In 1826, she left home to attend a Quaker boarding school in Providence, Rhode Island. She paid her way by teaching younger students and borrowing money from an older, married sister. In 1829, at the age of nineteen, she embarked on her adult life.

After spending a few years at home, Abby took a teaching job in Lynn, Massachusetts, where she heard the antislavery lectures of William Lloyd Garrison. She eagerly adopted his cause, which included not only the freeing of slaves, but the end of the slave trade and the granting of full civil rights for African Americans. These views, considered extreme at the time, made her an outcast. When she spoke against slavery, she was often refused entrance to churches and town halls, so she held meetings outdoors, in meadows and apple orchards, where she was pelted with rotten fruit and stones.

Abby was a moving and persuasive speaker. Her lively and independent spirit seeped into her speeches. Her oratory was so powerful that someone once told her that if she didn't keep speaking, "God will smite you."

But people still weren't used to women speaking in public, especially to audiences that included white men and African American people. On May 17, 1838, a mob of angry men gathered outside a newly built lecture hall in Philadelphia. Abby was among the antislavery speakers who addressed a crowd of three thousand people that afternoon. Despite the rising threat of violence, she and the other speakers, including Lucretia Mott, did not back down.

"It is the still small voice within, which may not be withstood, that bids me open my mouth for the dumb!" she shouted above the heckling men.

The women delivered their speeches and left the building, white women arm-in-arm with black women, pushing boldly through the swelling crowd. After they left, the mob rushed into the building, hacked it to pieces, and burned it to the ground. The building had stood for just four days!

In an odd twist of history, Abby led a series of antislavery meetings in Seneca Falls in 1843, five years before the women's rights convention was held there. She held nothing back—she accused

Suffragists spread

their message widely through speaking tours. Back then, lectures were a popular form of entertainment, as of course radios, movies, TVs, and phones hadn't been invented yet.

Lecturers were often backed by a speaker's bureau, called a lyceum, or by supporting organizations. The pay wasn't always good, but those who believed in a cause, like Abby, didn't mind the sacrifice—at first she even refused payment. Some lecturers, such as Lucretia Mott, came from well-to-do families, so money wasn't a concern. Others, like Sojourner Truth, sold books or cards printed with inspiring messages to add to their pay.

In the 1830s, Angelina and Sarah Grimké, two sisters from a southern slaveholding family, became the first women to speak publicly for the American Anti-Slavery Society. They suffered so much abuse for speaking in public that they began to speak out for women's rights. Following their example, the early suffragists gained the confidence to speak boldly in public for the ballot.

northerners of being as bad as southern slaveholders, because they had the power to end slavery but they would not. The audience became enraged—they threw rotten eggs, rum bottles, and worse at her. But that didn't stop her.

In the cause of suffrage, Abby went even further. "Harmony? I don't want harmony!" she said. "I want truth!" In 1873, she and her husband, Stephen Foster, refused to pay real estate taxes on their home in Worcester, Massachusetts. The government, they said, was made up entirely of men, and women had no role in electing them. That being the case, Abby reasoned, she didn't have to obey the law.

The Fosters' home was a stop on the Underground Railroad. After their deaths, its new owner renamed the home Liberty Farm. It is on the National Register of Historic Places.

The county seized the Fosters' property and set a public auction. Abby and her husband held a meeting to protest "taxation without representation"—a phrase they took from the Boston Tea Party of 1773, when American colonists protested taxes imposed by the British king.

At the meeting, suffragist Lucy Stone spoke up for her friend. "Now feeble by advancing age and by hard service for her country," she said, "tomorrow will have her house sold over her head because, like Jefferson and Adams and Hancock, she believes taxation without representation is tyranny."

Only one person bid, but he didn't bail out the Fosters. Instead of paying the bid price, he returned their home to the county, forcing another auction. At the second auction, the Fosters bought it back. Their protest went on for seven years and cost them their life savings.

Abby was a mentor for suffragists who came after her—she taught Lucy Stone and Susan B. Anthony how to speak forcefully, organize meetings, and raise funds. Many of the suffragist workers who joined the cause credited their inspiration to Abby. She never wanted women to forget the bravery of those who had paved the way for them. She was quick to remind them of their debt: "Bloody feet, Sisters, have worn smooth the path by which you come up hither."

The THINKING minds of ALL Nations call for CHANGE.

4

Elizabeth Cady Stanton

NOVEMBER 12, 1815–OCTOBER 26, 1902

THE RIGHT IS OURS.
HAVE IT, WE MUST. USE IT, WE WILL.

TEN-YEAR-OLD Elizabeth Cady watched in horror as her father, a lawyer in Johnstown, New York, told a weeping woman that he could not help her. Her husband had died and left nothing to her, even her home, which she had bought with money she had inherited. She was at the mercy of her son, who inherited everything and treated her poorly.

That night, Elizabeth grabbed a pair of scissors and sneaked into her father's office. She wanted to cut out the pages from the law book that had ruined the poor woman. Her father stopped her.

"When you are grown up," he said, "you must go down to Albany and talk to the legislators; tell them all you have seen in this office."

From an early age, Elizabeth was primed to rebel. She was one of eleven children, only five of whom survived to adulthood, all girls. When the last of her brothers died, her father was crushed. "Oh my daughter, I wish you were a boy!" he cried.

Elizabeth set out to become the child her father wanted—someone who was educated and brave, curious about the world, and informed about its issues. She pushed boundaries as an adult. When she married Henry Stanton, she did not vow to obey her husband, as brides of the time did. She called him by his first name, instead of Mr. Stanton, as wives did then. She didn't go by Mrs. Henry Stanton and she didn't abandon her maiden name. She was Elizabeth Cady Stanton. Period.

In 1840, Elizabeth met Lucretia Mott at the World Anti-Slavery Convention in London. Elizabeth was on her honeymoon and found that she enjoyed traveling and meeting new people.

Elizabeth took up scissors again when she wrote a controversial book, *The Woman's Bible*. She didn't like churches teaching that women were inferior to men. She cut and pasted Bible stories about women into a notebook. Next to these clippings, she wrote her own version.

Then came the awful moment when the male delegates voted to ban women from participating in the convention. Clergymen, in particular, "were in agony lest the women should do or say something to shock the heavenly hosts," Elizabeth scoffed.

But that didn't stop the women from airing their opinions. At hotels, on walks around the city, and in tea rooms, the women discussed their plight. In Lucretia Mott, Elizabeth found a mentor. Suddenly, Elizabeth saw the woman she could become.

Home life did consume much of Elizabeth's time. She had seven children and enjoyed being a mother, but she also felt like a prisoner. "I pace up and down these two chambers of mine like a caged lioness," she moaned.

In 1848, she was invited to join four other women at a friend's house in Seneca Falls, New York. There, she met up again with Lucretia Mott, and the women planned the 1848 Women's Rights Convention. Although the Declaration of Sentiments was a group effort, it is well known that Elizabeth was the main author. She knew how to inspire people with her words.

In October 1848, Elizabeth spoke at a suffrage convention in Waterloo, New York. Although the woman's vote had been hotly debated in Seneca Falls, it quickly became the main goal of the movement. Elizabeth's words became a rallying cry: "The right is ours. Have it, we must. Use it, we will."

Three years later, Elizabeth met Susan B. Anthony, and the two struck up a fierce, lifelong partnership. Elizabeth was the thinker and writer, Susan the speaker and organizer. Together, they became the driving force behind the suffrage movement. Side by side, they became icons of the cause—Susan tall and rail-thin, Elizabeth round and motherly.

Elizabeth and Susan drew crowds of women to the movement, but their extreme positions also alienated people. After the Civil War, as Congress considered granting African American men the vote, the two at first pushed for women and black men to be enfranchised at the same time. "As in the war, freedom was the keynote of victory, so now is universal suffrage the keynote of reconstruction," Elizabeth said. But in their zeal for the woman's cause, they began to openly slander African Americans.

No matter how much we love our friends, sometimes they can make us angry. It was the same for Elizabeth Cady Stanton and Susan B. Anthony. Despite their close relationship, they had epic arguments.

Being single and childless, Susan could devote herself entirely to the suffrage cause. She was often frustrated that Elizabeth's role as a wife and mother claimed her attention for long stretches of time. Elizabeth's sense of humor and easygoing nature often clashed with Susan's rigid and unbending character. Yet their friendship endured. "How I wish I could see you," Elizabeth once wrote to Susan, "even if to fight all the time."

The suffrage movement itself struggled with differences. When the Civil War broke out, some women wanted to focus solely on the war effort, while others wanted to continue the suffrage battle. After the war, women differed on whether to back the Fifteenth Amendment giving African American men the right to vote before women got it. In the 1860s, Susan and Elizabeth founded the National Woman Suffrage Association, which didn't want any more men getting the vote before women did, while Lucy Stone and Julia Ward Howe started the American Woman Suffrage Association, which supported the Fifteenth Amendment.

As the suffrage battle limped into the 1900s, women split again over tactics. Because a few states had approved the woman's vote, some suffragists wanted to continue lobbying state by state. Others worked for the federal amendment, wanting to gain a national victory and prevent states, particularly in the South, from depriving African Americans of the vote. In addition, some women became militant, picketing and disrupting political meetings, while others continued to politely lobby and persuade lawmakers.

Women were more deserving of the vote, Elizabeth declared, insulting black men as dirty, uneducated, and servile. Even as audience members cried out "Shame, shame, shame!" she would not relent.

Despite the controversy and ill will that Elizabeth caused, she continued to be a leader of the women's movement. She took her father's advice to make her demands known to elected officials on many occasions. In 1854, she spoke out for the vote before the New York State Legislature. In 1866, she ran for Congress, winning only two dozen votes but proving that women could run for office even if they could not vote. And on January 18, 1892, she brought her case to a committee of the U.S. House of Representatives. It was Elizabeth's words, written and spoken, that powered the early suffrage fight. The lioness had broken out of her cage.

Lucy Stone

AUGUST 13, 1818–OCTOBER 18, 1893

LEAVE WOMEN, THEN, TO FIND THEIR SPHERE.

AS A TEENAGER, Lucy Stone was part of a sewing circle that made clothes for local boys who attended college. One day, a pioneering educator named Mary Lyon visited the women and tried to interest them in starting a fund to send girls to college. Her effort was in vain.

At the end of the talk, Lucy folded up the shirt she was making and laid it on the table. She vowed she wouldn't sew one more seam of that shirt, or any other shirt, for a college boy. Why should she help boys to go to college when girls weren't allowed to attend?

Yes, Lucy was stubborn, but that quality served her well all her life.

Unafraid of her parents' opinion, Lucy announced one day that she would go to college. "Is the child crazy?" her father asked his wife. Lucy picked and sold berries and chestnuts to buy books to study for the entrance exam. She alternated studying with teaching, to earn more money. At twenty-five years old, she left Massachusetts and went off to Ohio's Oberlin College, the only mixed-gender college in the country.

At Oberlin, women's lowly status became clear to Lucy. To pay tuition, she took jobs cleaning common rooms and washing dishes. For chores, women were paid three cents an hour, while male students earned up to ten cents an hour. With her meager pay, Lucy could afford only fifty cents a week for food. She often went hungry.

Because of the injustices she experienced, Lucy worked to break down barrier after barrier. She chipped away at customs that prevented women from speaking in front of male students. She organized meetings for antislavery speakers, including

Abby Kelley and Stephen Foster. She studied and worked so hard that her father eventually agreed to support her.

But the inequity continued. She was chosen to write a speech for her class's graduation ceremony. There was a catch, though—speeches written by a woman had to be read by a man. Lucy declined.

In 1844, she was offered a teaching position at Oberlin, which paid 8 cents an hour. Yet again, she found that men made more than she did, earning 12.5 cents an hour. She resigned in protest. Her students pressured the college to do the right thing, and, after three months on strike, she won the higher rate.

Lucy's skill at persuasion powered her ability as a speaker. Her round face and open manner fooled people into thinking she was a pushover. In her first debate on whether women should vote, she faced off against a politician who was forced to admit that "that little blue-eyed girl in the calico gown . . . swept my arguments away like chaff before the wind."

In Lucy's day, one little-known state legislator voiced his support for suffrage. "I go for all sharing the privileges of the government who assist in bearing its burdens . . . by no means excluding females," said a young Abraham Lincoln.

One of Lucy's brothers, a pastor in Massachusetts, offered Lucy her first chance to lecture on women's rights. She delivered her speech, ignoring the hissing and stomping from male hecklers in the pews. When asked whether the hostility would put an end to her speaking career, she answered, "It only shows me how much work there is for me to do."

Lucy toured the country with the likes of Lucretia Mott and Abby Kelley Foster. She was pelted with spitballs and rotten vegetables and hosed with ice water. Yet she held her ground. Once, when she was being mobbed on stage, a man came at her with a club—she grabbed his upraised arm and, appealing to his sense of gallantry, convinced him to protect her instead.

Expanding the reach of the Seneca Falls convention, Lucy organized the first national women's rights convention, which was held in 1850 in Worcester, Massachusetts, and dozens of conventions afterward.

Lucy swore she would not marry, because to her marriage meant slavery. Even when she did eventually marry, at age thirty-seven, she kept her own last name rather than take the last name of her husband, Henry Blackwell. The couple rejected the customs that stripped married women of their rights, and she declined to be supported by Henry. She earned her own living throughout her life.

In 1857, the couple moved into a home in Orange, New Jersey, that belonged to Lucy. When the first tax bill came a few months later, they refused to pay it—fifteen years before Abby Kelley Foster staged her tax protest. The city sold some of her belongings to pay the bill, but friends bought everything back for her.

Lucy, along with her husband and Julia Ward Howe, cofounded the American Woman Suffrage Association in 1869. The next year, she began publishing *The Woman's Journal*, a weekly paper that aired women's views.

At a time when men decreed that women belonged in the home, Lucy worked for a woman's right to take whatever place she chose in society. "Leave women, then, to find their sphere," she said. "And do not tell us, before we are born even, that our province is to cook dinners, darn stockings and sew on buttons." For Lucy, the woman's sphere was the entire world, and she led the way in claiming it.

Today, many people

are vegetarians or vegans, but the idea of a plant-based diet is nothing new. In Lucy's time, the Graham System was all the rage.

In 1832, Sylvester Graham launched his innovative program for healthy living. He believed that you could prevent disease through a diet of vegetables, little to no meat, and whole-grain wheat flour. Have you ever had graham crackers? They're named after him! He discouraged the use of coffee, tea, alcohol, and tobacco. He urged people to wear loose clothing, exercise, take cold baths, and open their windows. He distrusted some medical practices, including bleeding patients and using medicines.

Starting in her college years, Lucy followed Graham's strict regimen. Other believers included Abby Kelley Foster, Angelina and Sarah Grimké, and Susan B. Anthony. Their self-discipline served them well, as suffragists often had to survive on the bare necessities of life while on the road drumming up support for the vote.

6

Julia Ward Howe

MAY 27, 1819–OCTOBER 17, 1910

MAKE YOUR PROTEST AGAINST TYRANNY, MEANNESS, AND INJUSTICE!

HAVE YOU EVER heard "The Battle Hymn of the Republic"? The words to this patriotic Civil War song were written by Julia Ward Howe. She was a poet and playwright who published her work despite her husband's disapproval.

Julia was born into a wealthy New York City family. Her father was a banker, but her mother died when Julia was five years old. Her father was kind, but stern and overprotective—Julia confided in her diary that she sometimes felt imprisoned in an enchanted castle.

Her father held traditional male views of femininity. As a young child, Julia once fell asleep on a carriage ride and her knees spread out on the seat. Her father scolded her. "My daughter, if you cannot sit still like a lady, we will stop at the next tailor's and have you measured for a pair of pantaloons!"

Julia was a pretty and talented young woman. Her delicate features, paired with her wit and charm, attracted so much male attention that her sisters called her "Diva Julia." She longed to be out in society, going to parties, concerts, and lectures, but her father forbade it. When she published her first piece, an anonymous essay, her uncle said, "This is my little girl who knows about books, and writes an article and has it printed, but I wish that she knew more about housekeeping."

At twenty-four, Julia married Samuel Gridley Howe, and they had six children. He was an abolitionist and founder of the Perkins School, a school for the blind in Massachusetts that still operates today. Yet while he championed enslaved and disabled people, he had no sympathy for women.

In the home, Samuel Howe was a dictator. He tried to stop Julia from writing, and he belittled and embarrassed her in public. The marriage was rocky, and the couple spent a lot of time apart. Julia poured out her anguish in *Passion-Flowers*, her first book of poems, which she published anonymously.

Among the shining I have shone,
Among the blessing, have been blest,
Then wearying years have held me bound
Where darkness deadness gives, not rest.

Julia was fifty years old when she joined the suffrage fight. Her husband tried to stop her, but she was determined to have her way. She regretted that she came so late to the cause. "Oh!" she said, "had I earlier known the power, the nobility, the intelligence which lie within the range of true womanhood, I had surely lived more wisely and to better purpose."

Female writers like Julia suffered the sting of male disapproval. They often wrote anonymously or under a pen name. Louisa May Alcott wrote twenty-nine stories as "A. M. Barnard" before she put her name on *Little Women* in 1868.

In 1869, Julia joined Lucy Stone in cofounding the American Woman Suffrage Association, a splinter group that wanted to see African American men get the vote, even if women had to wait. She edited *The Woman's Journal*, the newspaper Lucy founded. She took leading roles in women's suffrage organizations in New England and a wide array of women's clubs that worked for reform causes.

Julia's unhappy marriage ended with Samuel Howe's death in 1876. When they married, he had gained control of her inheritance, and, after he died, she found that through bad investments, he had lost most of it. He had left nothing in his will for her. Julia now fully understood the helplessness of being a woman without rights.

In Julia's circles, many people thought suffrage was a threat to the character of a true woman. They saw suffragists traveling without male escorts, speaking in public, shouting to be heard above jeering crowds, and cornering politicians with their demands. They condemned suffragists as crude and un-Christian. Julia fought this attitude. "The weapon of Christian warfare is the ballot," she said. "Adopt it, O you women, with clean hands and a pure heart!"

Julia's words to "The Battle Hymn of the Republic" called for justice for the enslaved. "As He died to make men holy, let us die to make men free," Julia wrote. In the same way, she saw the vote as the way to break free of societal slavery. "Make your protest against tyranny, meanness, and injustice!" she urged women. Julia's passion drew women of wealth and material comfort into the fight for women's suffrage.

Celebrities today

often lend their name to social concerns such as childhood hunger, literacy, or human trafficking. Their fame can bring attention and funds to these causes.

In the same way, famous women brought attention to the suffrage cause. These celebrities were generally actresses or wealthy women. A friend of the Howe family once said that Julia's great importance to the suffrage fight was that "she forms a bridge between the world of society and the world of reform."

Julia was just one of many celebrated women who fought for suffrage. Their family names are familiar even today—Tiffany, Astor, Vanderbilt, Rockefeller, Barrymore, Belmont. As managers of their homes and vast estates, these women knew how to organize. They enjoyed the limelight and knew their way around politics, business, and finance. They held fundraisers and financed suffrage conventions, parades, and offices. Their standing in society—and their money—allowed suffragists to carry their message to a wide audience.

7

Susan B. Anthony

FEBRUARY 15, 1820–MARCH 13, 1906

MEN, THEIR RIGHTS, AND NOTHING MORE; WOMEN, THEIR RIGHTS, AND NOTHING LESS.

SUSAN BROWNELL ANTHONY came home from school one day and told her parents that her teacher wouldn't let her learn long division. Girls didn't need to know advanced math, he'd told her. He might even have thought a girl's brain couldn't handle it!

Many people agreed with the teacher's view, but Susan's parents did not. They were Quakers who believed that men and women had equal abilities. They pulled her out of school and educated her in a school they started for local children. Susan was an eager student who went on to a Quaker boarding school when she was seventeen.

Susan's father owned a cotton mill in Battenville, New York, but in 1837 he lost the business in a recession. The family became innkeepers, housing and feeding travelers and mill workers. Their life was hard, but Susan did her part. "Baked 21 loaves of bread … wove three yards of carpet … got my quilt out of the frame … had 20 men to supper," she noted one day. She took a teaching job to help with her family's debts.

At her school, Susan found that male teachers earned $10 a month, while female teachers were paid only $2.50. She complained and was promptly fired. She taught elsewhere for a few more years, but eventually quit to take up reform causes. Dressed all in black, with glasses perched on her nose and hair pulled back into a bun, Susan cultivated a severe manner that suited her crusading role.

She began her activism with the temperance movement, which aimed to ban the sale of alcohol. But at rallies, she wasn't allowed to speak because she was a woman. One day, a legislator refused her temperance petition because the signatures were those of women. "I vowed then and there that women should be equal," she said.

Western New York State was a hotbed of social activism. In the early 1800s, it earned the nickname "The Burned-Over District," as a religious and reform movement known as the Second Great Awakening swept across the area like a forest fire.

Rochester was the home of both Susan B. Anthony and Frederick Douglass, who published an antislavery and women's rights newspaper called *The North Star*. Elizabeth Cady Stanton lived in Seneca Falls. Suffragist Matilda Joslyn Gage was from Cicero. Homer was the hometown of Amelia Bloomer, who published the first newspaper for women. Frances Willard, who founded the Woman's Christian Temperance Union, was born in Churchville. Florence Chauncey, the first woman to vote legally in New York State, cast her vote at 6:10 a.m. on January 5, 1918, in Lisle, New York, on the question of whether the town should be alcohol free. Rhoda Palmer, who signed the Declaration of Sentiments and voted at the age of 102 in the U.S. Senate elections in 1918, lived in Geneva.

Harriet Tubman, the former slave who conducted slaves to safety on the Underground Railroad, lived in Auburn. Emily Howland, who established schools for African American girls, was born in Sherwood. Margaret Sanger, who founded Planned Parenthood, was born in Corning. Clara Barton, the founder of the Red Cross, lived in Dansville. Clearly, the desire for change burned hot in the women of this region.

In 1851, Susan met Elizabeth Cady Stanton on a street corner in Seneca Falls, New York, three years after the women's convention there. It was the start of a fierce friendship and partnership that lasted more than fifty years.

In Elizabeth, Susan found someone who could put her thoughts into words. For the rest of her life, Susan traveled the country, speaking out for the vote. In 1868, the two women started a magazine, *The Revolution*, into which they poured their opinions. Its masthead proclaimed: "Men, their rights, and nothing more; women, their rights, and nothing less." Their views on women's rights were so radical for the time that *The New York Times* called *The Revolution* "literary nitroglycerin."

In letters to friends, Susan wrote passionately about the vote. "Now wouldn't it be splendid for us to be free & equal citizens, with the power of the ballot to back our hearts, heads & hands?" she wrote to a friend.

Susan's strong personality and rigid opinions caused some rifts. For a while, the movement, which had started as the American Equal Rights Association, split apart into the National Woman Suffrage Association and the American Woman Suffrage Association. The two groups differed on whether African American men should get the vote before women did. Susan and Elizabeth opposed the Fifteenth Amendment, not because it gave the vote to African American men, but because it didn't grant the vote to women at the same time. To give the vote to all men and deny it to all women, they said, was to create an "aristocracy of sex."

But eventually their stand became racist. The most intelligent class of people should get the vote first, Susan declared, so therefore, "Let woman be first and the negro last."

Opponents countered that it was immoral for women to claim they had a greater need for the vote. "When women, because they are women . . . are dragged from their homes and are hung from lamp-posts; when their children are torn from their arms, and their brains bashed out upon the pavement . . . then they will have an urgency to obtain the ballot equal to our own," protested their great friend and ally, Frederick Douglass, the escaped slave and abolitionist.

After the Fifteenth Amendment passed in 1870, Susan pleaded with people to finally see the justice of the woman's vote: "Put into the hands of all women, as you have into those of all men, the ballot, that symbol of perfect equality, that right protective of all other rights." To that end, Susan continued her relentless campaign for the vote.

Susan's most memorable act came on November 5, 1872, when she went into a barbershop in Rochester, New York, to vote in a presidential election. It was illegal, Susan knew, but she hoped her action would bring the suffrage fight to the courts. She convinced the male registrars to allow her and fourteen other women to vote. "Well, I have been & gone & done it!!" she wrote excitedly to Elizabeth.

All was quiet for about three weeks. But then a marshal showed up at Susan's house to arrest her. She went gladly—even holding out her hands to be handcuffed. Ashamed to be arresting a woman, the marshal wouldn't do it. They took a trolley to the police station, which delighted Susan, who loudly made known her plight. Susan was tried, found guilty, and given a $100 fine. She refused to pay it, yet the judge wouldn't jail her. He wanted to keep the matter from going on to higher courts.

Susan lived for thirty-two years after her act of rebellion, with woman suffrage still not in sight. Adorned in a red silk shawl, she haunted the halls of power. In 1878, she was among a group of women who first proposed an amendment to the Constitution. It came to be known as the Susan B. Anthony Amendment. She never gave up hope. In her last public outing, she praised the young women who were carrying on the fight, certain that they would complete what her generation had started. "Failure is impossible!" she insisted.

It is the plain Duty of every Woman to desire to VOTE, and of every man to Remove the obstacles in her way.

8

Isabella Beecher Hooker

FEBRUARY 22, 1822–JANUARY 25, 1907

CAN ANYTHING BE PLAINER
THAN THAT A WOMAN,
BEING A "PERSON," IS A CITIZEN?

ISABELLA BEECHER HOOKER lived in the shadow of a famous sister. Her older sister, Harriet, had written *Uncle Tom's Cabin*, a powerful novel that shed light on the horrors of slavery. After the book's publication in 1852, only the Bible sold more copies than Harriet Beecher Stowe's book.

But it was another piece of writing that stirred Isabella's heart. One day in 1859, she read a magazine article titled "Ought Women to Learn the Alphabet?" Education was an issue close to Isabella's heart—her own had been spotty and uninspiring. The writer pointed out the flaw in thinking that women could be educated to a point, but not attend college. That women could sing in public, but not speak in public. And, most bitingly, that women could drop a piece of paper into a mailbox, but not a ballot box.

Isabella was so dazzled that she wrote the author a fan letter. She was thrilled when he wrote back! Thomas Wentworth Higginson urged her to follow in the footsteps of women who held the same beliefs, women like Lucretia Mott, Elizabeth Cady Stanton, and Lucy Stone.

It was many years before Isabella took that advice. At the time, she was married and raising three children. She was leading the same conventional life she had seen her own mother live. She had grown up in a household crammed with children, first in Connecticut and then Ohio. Her brothers had all gone to college, while she and

In 1882, Isabella's husband, John Hooker, successfully argued before the Connecticut Supreme Court that women should be admitted to the state bar, the licensing body for lawyers. His apprentice, Mary Hall, became the first woman to practice law in Connecticut.

her sisters had dipped in and out of school. Her father, the famous preacher Lyman Beecher, didn't think much of educating girls.

Isabella yearned for a life of learning. In 1841 she married a lawyer, John Hooker, and often would take her knitting to his office so they could read together. One day, he read from a law book that explained how upon marriage a woman loses her legal identity—*how she no longer exists*. Isabella argued the point, but at last dropped it as "a hopeless mystery."

Although Isabella hadn't taken Higginson's advice to join the women's rights movement right away, she did write her own article just one year after his. In "Shall Women Vote?" she argued that women have enough life experience as wives, mothers, and household managers to be intelligent voters. But still, she straddled the fence. "I would not open the polls to women today—no, nor next year, nor ever, unless public opinion demanded it." She was not ready to act yet, but the idea of woman suffrage had been planted in her mind.

In 1869, ten years after she read Higginson's words, Isabella began writing to Elizabeth Cady Stanton and Susan B. Anthony, and finally she heard them speak. Now she was ready to take Higginson's advice. "With equal political rights come equal social and industrial opportunities," she wrote, promising to work with the suffragists.

In the suffrage cause, Isabella's sister Harriet became her role model. "My sister's book, 'Uncle Tom's Cabin,' . . . had such an influence in the abolition cause that it gave me an incentive to do the best I could to emancipate women," she said.

Isabella regretted the rift in the suffrage movement that pitted suffragists against each other. She wanted to unite the two sides that had split over whether African American men should gain the vote before women. In 1870, the Fifteenth Amendment granting African American men the vote had passed, but the suffrage groups continued to work separately.

Isabella presided over a convention in 1871 in which she tried to mend fences, urging everyone to agree that the Constitution, speaking as it did of "people," already granted women the right to vote. "Can anything be plainer than that a woman, being a 'person,' is a citizen, and being a 'citizen' has the citizen's right to vote?" she asked.

The suffrage groups didn't reunite until 1890, but Isabella got the process started.

Isabella's greatest triumph came in gaining married women the right to own property in her home state. For eight years, she tried to persuade the Connecticut General Assembly to consider a bill granting that right. Finally, in 1877, it passed, and women in Connecticut no longer had to turn over their property to their husbands.

Isabella never let up on suffrage. Every year until 1901, she presented a suffrage bill before the Connecticut General Assembly. In 1893, she persuaded several U.S. senators to back a limited national suffrage proposal. Women—Isabella's people, her citizens—were getting closer to the vote.

Families often argue,

and Isabella's family was no different. She and her siblings fought over issues big and small.

Isabella worked to gain the vote, but her sister Catharine declared that women didn't need it. Their job was to be the moral, stable heart of the family. It bothered Isabella that Catharine wanted to limit women's lives, especially since Catharine was single and childless and never had a home of her own. The family also had a falling-out over charges that Isabella's brother Henry, a famous preacher like his father, had had an affair with a married woman. In the resulting scandal and trial, some of the siblings maintained he was innocent, while Isabella insisted he was guilty and pressed him to confess.

Later in Isabella's life, the family became alarmed about her belief in Spiritualism. Spiritualists thought that spirits from beyond the grave could speak, give advice, and see the future. Isabella attended séances, put up shrines to dead loved ones, and claimed to channel their words. Some family members limited contact with her or, at times, completely disowned her, but most of the family reconciled with Isabella before her death.

Millions of colored WOMEN today Share with colored men THE responsibilities of FREEDOM.

9

Mary Ann Shadd Cary

OCTOBER 9, 1823–JUNE 5, 1893

WHO SHALL OVERRULE
THE VOICE OF WOMAN?

REBEL, THEY CALLED HER. Mischief maker. Agitator.

Yes, Mary Ann Shadd was all that and so much more.

One day, Frederick Douglass watched her make her way along a New York City street. He couldn't help but sing her praises.

"Coming down Broadway at a time when colored women hardly dared to think of riding in public trolleys, M. A. Shadd threw up her head, gave one look and a wave of her hand." Her manner was such that a trolley driver, "a large, coarse, ruffianly man" not known to stop for African American women, brought his team of horses to a halt, "suddenly seized with paralysis."

Mary Ann had that effect on people!

Mary Ann was the child of freed slaves. The family was large—she was one of thirteen children. Although they were middle class, she could not be educated in Delaware, where they lived. Some public schools educated black children, but they enrolled only boys. So the family moved to Pennsylvania, where they settled in Quaker country outside of Philadelphia.

Education wasn't the only issue that prompted the move. In Delaware, people were talking about deporting black people—enslaved or free—to Africa. Mary Ann's father had no intention of letting that happen. He became active in efforts to ensure that black people could live where they wanted to.

Mary Ann was ten years old when the family moved. She attended a Quaker school and lived comfortably on a farm amid a growing free black community. The family's house became a stop on the Underground Railroad. But Delaware called her back—as a teacher, she wanted to make sure all black children could be educated in that state.

After teaching in Delaware, and later in two other states, Mary Ann became impatient for black people to build better lives. Even in the North, she noted, prejudice was everywhere. She wrote a letter to Frederick Douglass. "We should do more, and talk less," she said. He published her letter in his newspaper, *The North Star*.

More alarming was Congress's passing in 1850 of the Fugitive Slave Act, which allowed white slave owners to track down escaped slaves and drag them back down south. But slave owners weren't stopping at that—even free black men and women were being snatched off the streets. Mary Ann thought the solution was to move to Canada, where she believed that blacks could prosper.

In 1883, at the age of sixty, Mary Ann earned her law degree from Howard University School of Law. She was the second black woman in the United States to become a lawyer, earning her degree eleven years after Charlotte E. Ray.

In Canada, Mary Ann again took up teaching and in 1853 started a newspaper for the black community called *The Provincial Freeman*. In doing so, she became the first African American woman to found a newspaper in North America. The paper struggled to stay afloat on subscriptions and donations. One day, Mary Ann opened an envelope and was delighted to find a generous donation from Lucretia Mott!

In 1856, Mary Ann married a barber named Thomas Cary, had two children, and for several decades worked tirelessly for the cause of racial uplift. She didn't want charity from white people—she wanted her people to work hard to better their own lives.

In the waning days of the Civil War, she was asked to help enlist African American regiments to fight for the Union. In the late 1860s, she moved to Washington, DC, where she began to work for suffrage alongside Susan B. Anthony and Elizabeth Cady Stanton. In 1874, she was among a group of handpicked suffragists who spoke before the House Judiciary Committee. "Millions of colored women today share with colored men the responsibilities of freedom," she told the committee.

On election day that year, Mary Ann and sixty-three other women headed for the polls to try to vote. When workers refused to register them, the women demanded

When it came to the vote, bias was everywhere. White men wanted to keep it for themselves. And white women weren't free from prejudice either.

"'Better whiskey and more of it!' is the rallying cry of great, dark-faced mobs," temperance reformer and suffragist Frances Willard said, insulting the character of African Americans.

"Think of Patrick and Sambo and Hans and Yung Tung, who do not know the difference between a monarchy and a republic, who cannot read the Declaration of Independence or Webster's spelling-book, making laws for Lucretia Mott, Ernestine L. Rose, and Anna E. Dickinson," scoffed Elizabeth Cady Stanton, slurring immigrants and African Americans alike.

"For all these ignorant, alien peoples, educated American-born women have been compelled to stand aside and wait!" groused Susan B. Anthony. Suffragist leader Alice Paul dreamed of retiring to the country where there were still "some American people left."

Whole classes of people were judged unworthy of the vote, including Native Americans, people who couldn't read or write, African Americans, and immigrants. Suffragists were too often willing to play to people's racist beliefs in their pursuit of suffrage support. It is a blot on their records that cannot be erased.

sworn statements that they had been turned away. Mary Ann wasn't about to slink home quietly.

In 1878, in a speech at the National Woman Suffrage Association convention, Mary Ann tied the issue of the vote to the action of political parties, one of the early suffragists to make that connection. "Mary A. S. Cary, a worthy representative of the District of Columbia . . . said the colored women would support whatever party would allow them their rights, be it Republican or Democrat," the record showed.

Mary Ann believed that black women needed to take leadership roles in their communities. Only then would jobs, education, and better living conditions follow. And it would all start with the vote. "Who shall overrule the voice of woman?" she asked. In her world, no one could.

I think I was born with a HATRED of oppression.

Matilda Joslyn Gage

MARCH 24, 1826–MARCH 18, 1898

THE SOUL MUST ASSERT
ITS OWN SUPREMACY OR DIE.

HAVE YOU EVER heard the saying, "Children should be seen and not heard"? Some adults think children should speak only when they are spoken to. Otherwise they should stay out of the conversation of adults, and out of their way.

That wasn't the way it was in Matilda Joslyn's house. She was an only child whose parents wanted her to think for herself. Her opinions were considered, and every question she asked was answered. Her father, a doctor in Cicero, New York, took her on his rounds and taught her Greek, math, and science. To learn about anatomy and the systems of the body, she helped him dissect small animals.

The slavery debate raged throughout Matilda's childhood. The Joslyn house was a stop on the Underground Railroad. Her abolitionist feelings were fanned into flame when she heard Abby Kelley Foster speak. She began handing out pamphlets and asking people to sign petitions. "I think I was born with a hatred of oppression," she said.

At age eighteen, Matilda married Henry H. Gage, a shopkeeper, and they had four children. Their home in Fayetteville, New York, became a center for reform activity. Matilda championed the rights of African Americans, workers, and women. In 1852, she gave her first speech at a women's rights convention in Syracuse. She was twenty-six years old and the youngest person to speak—she stood on the platform holding her daughter's hand. Tall and graceful, she spoke hesitantly at first, but gained confidence as she went along.

Unlike suffragists whose faith formed the basis of their activism, Matilda blamed religion for limiting women's lives. After the Syracuse convention, a newspaper editor called the gathering "satanic." A local minister wrote a letter to the editor outlining his anti-suffrage views. Matilda struck back in the newspaper, signing herself as "M." The debate raged between "M" and the minister until finally he demanded to know who he was debating. Readers were surprised to learn that it was a woman using history, philosophy, religion, and literature to make her points.

When it came to women's place in society, Matilda didn't have to look far for inspiration. She lived in central New York State, side-by-side with Native American communities. She became fascinated with their way of life, which didn't force women to beg for respect.

Matilda's son-in-law, L. Frank Baum, wrote *The Wonderful Wizard of Oz*, a book made famous by the 1939 movie, *The Wizard of Oz*. Baum's books often featured women in nontraditional roles. In many of his stories, myths of who holds power are shattered, such as when the wizard is shown to be an ordinary man.

In 1875, while she was president of the National Woman Suffrage Association, Matilda wrote a series of articles on the Iroquois tribes of central New York for the *New York Evening Post*. She wanted our government to be like theirs, with women and men participating equally. "Never was justice more perfect, never civilization higher," Matilda wrote. She spent the rest of her life writing about Native American societies.

To honor Matilda, the Mohawk nation adopted her into the Wolf Clan in 1893 and gave her the name Ka-ron-ien-ha-wi, meaning "She who holds the sky." As a member, Matilda could vote on tribal matters, including the naming of its chief.

How ironic that honor was! In 1871, Matilda had been turned away when she tried to vote in her local school board election. She could vote in her adopted nation, but not in her birth nation. She was determined to change that.

From 1878 to 1881, Matilda owned and edited a suffrage newspaper, *The National Citizen and Ballot Box*. In it, she wrote essays about women's issues regarding not only the vote, but the home, marriage, church, and societal customs. Each issue was headed with the motto, "The Pen Is Mightier than the Sword."

In 1893, she wrote the book that became her legacy, *Woman, Church and State*. In it, she described how she believed that throughout history, the Christian faith and its male leaders had conspired to oppress women.

Through Matilda's leadership, New York State granted women the right to vote for school board members in 1880. On the first election day, she staked out the polls to make sure women were not turned away. Yet, in 1893, New York took away that right—educators were unhappy that women were electing female board members.

Matilda, a frail woman who had heart trouble all her life, died just two years before the dawning of the 1900s, a new century in which a third generation of women would need to continue the fight. But Matilda's words rang out still—"The soul must assert its own supremacy or die!"— guiding them with her call for women to take their rightful place in society.

 Elizabeth Cady Stanton, Susan B. Anthony, and Matilda Joslyn Gage wrote a huge book about the suffrage movement. Their *History of Woman Suffrage* was published in three volumes and was three thousand pages long. Still, it covered the movement only up to 1885! Three more volumes were added in the 1900s by Ida Husted Harper and other women working for the National American Woman Suffrage Association.

Were suffragists dreaming up something new when they called for women to have a say in government and society? Hardly!

For hundreds of years, Native Americans had lived in the Seneca Falls area. The Haudenosaunee, an alliance of six Iroquois tribes, lived alongside white communities. Lucretia Mott visited the Cattaraugus, a Seneca tribe, a month before the Seneca Falls convention. Elizabeth Cady Stanton was known to bless a meal saying, "Heavenly Father and Mother," addressing a female deity as Native Americans would. She would have met them through her cousin, the abolitionist Gerrit Smith, who freely invited Native Americans into his home. Matilda was working on a book about the Haudenosaunee when she died.

The Haudenosaunee were a matriarchal society, one that was ruled by women. Women held property and passed it down through their families, and children were part of the mother's clan. Women could choose the kind of work they wanted to do, and communal work was overseen by women. Laws were made with input from women. The right to rule was passed down through a wife's family. Tribal chiefs were chosen and removed by women. Treaties made between tribes needed the approval of women, and women could end treaties or veto war. In this society, women held the power.

11
Frances Willard

SEPTEMBER 28, 1839–FEBRUARY 17, 1898

THE GUNS ARE BALLOTS AND
THE BULLETS ARE IDEAS.

ONE DAY when she was a child, Frances Willard's brother Oliver challenged her to walk ahead of him across a pasture. Simple! But there was a catch—he was holding a loaded double-barreled shotgun aimed at her with both barrels cocked. She marched boldly across the field, not afraid for one second.

Frances Willard was not one to refuse a dare.

Frances considered herself a wild child. She grew up on a farm in Wisconsin and was allowed to run free. She played all the games boys did—marbles, tops, horseshoes. She walked on stilts and climbed trees. She learned how to use tools and made her own wooden carts, sleds, bows and arrows, and other toys. It's no surprise that she was called a tomboy!

Her childhood taught her an early lesson about women's rights. "It is good for boys and girls to know the same things, so that the former shall not feel and act so overwise," she said.

The day that Frances turned sixteen was the day she called her martyrdom. From then on, she was forced into the costume of a woman. Gone were her short hair, loose dresses, and sturdy shoes. In their place, she wore corsets, petticoats, long and heavy skirts, buttoned shoes, ribboned bonnets, and gloves. She had to pin up her hair using eighteen hairpins. Outdoor activities became impossible—even walking was a chore.

But Frances had a lively mind, and she loved learning. Until she was eleven, her education came mostly from her family and neighbors. Her mother taught her to read poetry aloud with confidence and emotion. It prepared her well for her life as a public speaker. She graduated in 1859 from a women's college in Evanston, Illinois.

Frances became a teacher, despite her father's disapproval. He had been a modern father—he had always played with his children and had cared for them whenever his wife was away—but he thought only a man should work. Frances disagreed. "Girls should be definitely set at work after their school days end, even as boys are, to learn some bread-winning employment that will give them an independent status," she protested.

A famous painting features Frances Willard surrounded by outcasts of society considered unworthy of the vote—prisoners, Native Americans, and those who were called lunatics and idiots. It debased many groups of people by implying that unlike them, women were worthy of the vote.

In 1874, Frances left teaching, even though she'd risen to become dean of the women's college of Northwestern University. Activism called to her. As a girl, she'd heard Abby Kelley Foster speak against slavery, a memory that stayed with her. She dedicated herself to the temperance cause, as she saw alcohol abuse destroying family life through violence and poverty.

Frances helped found the Woman's Christian Temperance Union that year, eventually becoming its president. She worked tirelessly to gain both the public's support and the backing of political candidates. Sometimes, she gave more than four hundred speeches a year.

Soon, she saw that if women had the vote, they could enact laws to ban alcohol and veto liquor licenses. Unlike other suffragists, Frances didn't frame suffrage as a right. She saw it as a means to an end. In what she called the "home protection" fight, she said "the guns are ballots and the bullets are ideas."

Susan B. Anthony was thrilled when Frances joined the suffrage cause. The WCTU was a huge organization with a national reach. But not every temperance worker wanted suffrage. "We do not propose to trail our skirts through the mire of politics," sniffed one WCTU leader.

But politics held no scorn for Frances. If women were in politics, she said, they could walk side by side with men "clad in the garments of power!"

Frances had a natural talent for persuading, negotiating, and compromising. She loved the limelight, even though she considered it a sin. She was modest, generally dressing in black or gray, but she wore sky blue scarves that drew people's eyes to her. She had a gentle, pleasing manner and freely showed concern and affection for others. She knew exactly how to work a room.

The suffrage fight

was slowed by differing opinions on many fronts. But when it came to one issue—religion—suffragists were willing to put aside their differences.

Lucretia Mott and Susan B. Anthony were Quakers. Frances Willard was a Methodist. Two other suffrage leaders, Adelina Otero-Warren and Lucy Burns, were Catholic. Mary Ann Shadd Cary's religion was education, and Matilda Joslyn Gage followed no religion at all. Suffragists worked alongside Pandita Ramabai Sarasvati, a Hindu woman who worked for better lives for women and children in India. They welcomed volunteer Komako Kimura, a Japanese actress and wife of a self-styled spiritual teacher. And they helped Jewish women defeat anti-Semitic, anti-suffrage political candidates.

"I find great good in all religions . . . no word of faith in God or love toward man is alien to my sympathy," Frances Willard declared. Elizabeth Cady Stanton agreed. "I can speak and work with all the children of men," she wrote to Isabella Beecher Hooker. For suffragists, it seems, the only religion that mattered was faith in woman herself.

But Frances was another suffragist who stooped to slandering black people in her pursuit of the vote. In the South, she brazenly proclaimed that black people were drunkards and black men a menace to white women. Suffragist Ida B. Wells-Barnett was incensed. Frances Willard insulted the entire black community "in order to gain favor with those who are hanging, shooting and burning Negroes alive," she accused. Frances's words were an unexpected slap in the face, as many WCTU chapters freely admitted black people. She lost the support of many women over her racist stance, but still she remained in the thick of the suffrage fight.

Frances pushed for other changes in women's lives. In her fifties, she took up bicycling, an activity that was considered unladylike and even a threat to women's health. On a bicycle, she could shed some of her hated clothing and enjoy the outdoors once again. Her book on learning how to ride a bicycle, *Wheel Within a Wheel*, became a best seller and encouraged women to hit the road.

Frances rallied a huge and passionate following to the suffrage cause. For women, she wanted total freedom—to work, to live peaceably in their homes, to vote and participate in politics, to move freely in the world. At her death, she even defied the burial customs of the day, insisting she be cremated and her ashes returned to the earth she so loved.

12

Anna Howard Shaw

FEBRUARY 14, 1847–JULY 2, 1919

IN THE PEOPLE'S VOICE THERE IS A SOPRANO AS WELL AS A BASS.

IT WAS a pitch-black night in the forest, and Anna Howard Shaw, a newly minted Methodist minister, jostled up and down on a horse-drawn wagon. The driver was making her uneasy with his lurid stories and coarse laugh. But she had to get to a lumber camp in northern Michigan by morning to preach a sermon. A few miles into the twenty-two-mile journey, he stopped the cart.

"I'll be damned if I take you," he said. "I've got you here, and I'm going to keep you here!"

At that, Anna pulled a revolver out of her purse, cocked it, and aimed it at the driver's back. "Drive on," she said.

Anna arrived safely at her destination.

Anna Howard Shaw knew how to survive. When she was just twelve years old, her father had dropped off his wife and five of their children at a rough-hewn, dirt-floor cabin in the Michigan woods, leaving them to fend for themselves. They were one hundred miles from the railroad and forty miles from the nearest town. "He gave no thought to the manner in which we were to make the struggle and survive the hardships before us," Anna said. The forsaken family would shiver in their freezing cabin, cowering as the howling of wolves cut through the night air.

Anna was up to the challenge. She learned how to fell trees, cut wood, dig a well, plow and plant crops, hunt, fish, and cook over an open fire. But she had a dreamy side, too. She pored over the snippets of newspapers they'd pasted to the walls of their cabin to keep out the cold. She'd walk out to a clearing in the woods, step up onto a tree stump, and preach sermons to the trees.

The first time Anna spoke to a large audience, she was so terrified she fainted. Despite protests from her friends, she returned to the podium ten minutes later and started again, this time making it through to the end.

As many teen girls did, Anna took up teaching to help support the family while her father and brothers were fighting in the Civil War. But in 1870, wanting to earn more, she moved in with a married sister in Big Rapids, Michigan, and became a seamstress. One fateful day only a month after she'd arrived, she heard a sermon by a visiting Universalist preacher—a woman. "It was a wonderful moment when I saw my first woman minister enter her pulpit," she said. The minister urged her to go back to school.

With the backing of her sister and brother-in-law, Anna made her way through high school. She began preaching almost immediately, and in 1871, at the age of twenty-four, she was named one of the first woman preachers in the Methodist Church. From her first sermon onward, Anna's presence in the pulpit was like "a lighted match applied to gunpowder." So strong was the view of the day that women should not be ministers that Anna's own family became estranged from her for a while.

In 1873, Anna went on to attend Albion College in Michigan, Boston University's School of Theology, and Boston Medical School, where she earned a doctorate in medicine. She paid her way through school by giving temperance lectures and preaching. Sometimes she was paid, sometimes not. She was at the point of starvation many times—the wolf was howling at her door, just as in her childhood.

Anna met many of the great reform speakers—Frances Willard, Julia Ward Howe, and Lucy Stone among them. In 1885, she resigned from her church positions to join the suffrage cause. As a pastor, she had seen women who were virtual slaves in their own homes, underpaid and unsafe in their workplaces, and victims of male ridicule and violence. The real work of her life had begun.

In Anna's view, democracy demanded equality. "In the people's voice, there is a soprano as well as a bass," she insisted.

In 1888, Anna began working with sixty-eight-year-old Susan B. Anthony. They traveled thousands of miles and endured harsh frontier conditions to drum up support for suffrage. No bed to sleep on? Bread and watermelon for dinner and only raisins for breakfast? A blizzard blowing in or mud tugging at your skirts? That was nothing to a pioneer woman.

Yet even Anna needed encouragement once in a while. She often drew strength from the older woman. To Susan, "the hardships we underwent . . . were as the airiest trifles," she said.

Anna played a key role in bringing together the suffragists who split over the issue of African American males voting. The National Woman Suffrage Association and American Woman Suffrage Association had finally merged in 1890 under the leadership of Susan B. Anthony. Anna was president of the merged National American Woman Suffrage Association for eleven years, handing over the reins to Carrie Chapman Catt in 1915.

When Anna wrote her memoirs that year, she saw victory ahead. "I have not yet won the great and vital fight of my life, to which I have given myself, heart and soul, for the past thirty years—the campaign for woman suffrage. . . . But when the ultimate triumph comes— when American women in every state cast their ballots as naturally as their husbands do—I may not be in this world to rejoice over it."

Indeed, Anna did not live to see victory, but she came achingly close. She died on July 2, 1919, just two days before Congress finally passed the Nineteenth Amendment. The triumph she had tirelessly worked for did indeed come.

In the suffrage fight,

there were bass voices as well as soprano ones. Much of the credit for the full chorus goes to Anna Howard Shaw.

At Anna's urging, several prominent men formed the Men's League for Woman Suffrage in 1909. James Lees Laidlaw, a banker and the husband of suffragist Harriet Burton Laidlaw, was the league's president. He organized male delegations to march in suffrage parades. Max Eastman, a reformer who had grown up in a suffrage household, spoke on college campuses and helped students form suffrage associations. By 1912, the league boasted twenty thousand members.

Forming a league was key to drawing men to the cause. "There are many men who inwardly feel the justice of equal suffrage, but who are not ready to acknowledge it publicly, unless backed by numbers," Laidlaw said. These men endured taunts and bullying just as female suffragists did. During parades, onlookers jeered them—"Henpecko!" or "Hold up your skirts, girls!" As one member said: "Tagging after the girls—that's what we were doing; and nobody would let us forget it." But the men held their ground.

13

Carrie Chapman Catt

JANUARY 9, 1859–MARCH 9, 1947

WE WOMEN DEMAND AN EQUAL VOICE; WE SHALL ACCEPT NOTHING LESS.

CARRIE LANE had an early interest in politics. Raised on a farm in Iowa, she went with her father to campaign rallies for Horace Greeley, who was running for president against Ulysses S. Grant in 1872. When her cat had a litter of kittens, Carrie named them for Greeley, Grant, and their running mates!

On Election Day, Carrie's father, brother, and farmhands hitched up a wagon to head for town. Carrie was puzzled that her mother wasn't getting ready to go. "Why, Mother, aren't you going to vote for Greeley?" she asked. At that, everyone laughed. Everyone but Carrie knew that women couldn't vote.

After finishing high school, Carrie passed her college exams and earned her teaching certificate—all without telling her parents. She'd read Charles Darwin's new book, *On the Origin of Species*, and was convinced that humans could evolve in moral and intellectual ways, becoming ever higher beings. She was sure college would help her evolve.

At Iowa State College, Carrie was struck by the college's military-style training program for men. Women weren't offered any physical activity. She convinced the college to let her start "G Company," which gave girls an opportunity for exercise. She also defied the rule that allowed only men to speak in the debate club.

Upon graduating in 1880, Carrie was offered a job as principal of a school in Mason City, Iowa. When she arrived, they told her they could only offer her the assistant principal's job. Carrie was defiant—she said she'd take the top job or nothing. They gave her the promised position.

Carrie knew success

would only come with a wide base of support, so she got creative about spreading the suffrage message.

Suffragists shouted their views from soapboxes in the street. On Mother's Day, they pressured preachers to give pro-suffrage sermons. On the Fourth of July, suffragists read the Declaration of Sentiments from courthouse steps. On Labor Day, they enlisted labor leaders to speak at workers' picnics. They tacked up posters in store windows and traipsed across fields to talk to farmers. They flung leaflets from biplanes. One artist attracted crowds by sketching while she promoted suffrage. Another woman spoke between bouts at a prize fight in Madison Square Garden. Carrie made sure the newspapers knew about every stunt.

Suffragists were mocked as bitter, ugly "she-men." They were often depicted in cartoons looking like "escapers from the insane asylums." One vile sideshow entertainer exhibited a four-hundred-pound teenage girl as a supposed specimen of how women would look if they had rights. So it is fitting that one of their most successful tactics was the "suffrage cafe." Attractive young women circulated among patrons at these pop-up restaurants, serving up lunch with a side of suffrage propaganda.

In 1885, she married Leo Chapman, the editor of the Mason City newspaper, and became its coeditor. When Leo died of typhoid fever in California the next year, Carrie moved there and took another newspaper job. Returning to Iowa a year later, she took her third job in journalism. Yet just as women do today, she suffered sexual harassment in the workplace—she had to fight off men when they tried to "scrape acquaintance" with her.

When Carrie returned to Iowa in 1887, she began campaigning for women's right to vote in local elections. Invited to a statewide suffrage meeting in 1889, she was intrigued by a quiet, gray-haired woman in a lace cap—it was Lucy Stone.

Carrie came on the suffrage scene just when suffragists were becoming discouraged. They couldn't convince states to adopt suffrage or lawmakers to consider the federal amendment. Carrie energized the flagging movement with her gift for organizing and ability to mobilize groups, especially young people. She was a tall, dignified woman with a full-throated voice perfect for speech-making. "I have a voice like a foghorn!" she used to say. People paid attention to Carrie.

In 1900, when she became president of the National American Woman Suffrage Association, she pinned a map of the United States on her office wall.

It was color-coded to show the states in which women had full suffrage and could vote in all local and national elections, those in which a limited suffrage allowed them to vote in some local or congressional elections, and states that had no woman suffrage at all. She wanted to see full suffrage splashed across the map. "We women demand an equal voice; we shall accept nothing less," she declared.

She resigned as NAWSA president in 1904 to promote world suffrage, but her resignation was also personal—her second husband, George Catt, was dying. He was a huge supporter of her work, and she was heartbroken. "My husband needs me now . . . and I will not leave him," she said.

But the national effort sagged again, and NAWSA called her back in 1915. The next year, Carrie organized an emergency convention in Atlantic City, New Jersey, to revive the dying movement. "The Woman's Hour has struck!" she declared. "Women arise: Demand the vote!"

Part of Carrie's "Winning Plan" was to gain suffrage in New York State. On October 23, 1915, she led a parade of fifty thousand people down Fifth Avenue. Finally, people seemed to under-

Suffragists honored Carrie with the gift of a sapphire- and diamond-studded brooch. Teachers asked children to bring pennies to school for the pin. One boy asked his puzzled mother for a penny for "Charlie Chaplin's cat"!

stand the depth of the suffragists' passion. "This is not a movement; it is not a campaign; this is a crusade!" one man said. It took two more years, but in 1917, New York granted women the vote. By 1919, fifteen states had granted women full suffrage, and in another twenty states, women could vote in school board or local elections.

Carrie's skillful political activism pushed suffrage over its final hurdles. Her drive for state-by-state suffrage and later for the federal amendment endured setback after setback, but because of her, millions of people joined the fight, legislators reversed course, and President Woodrow Wilson, who had been on the fence, finally urged Congress to back the amendment.

When on June 4, 1919, the Nineteenth Amendment finally made it through Congress, Carrie's was the loudest voice of triumph. "You've won! Be glad! Rejoice, applaud and be glad!" she cried. And in August 1920, when the states voted to add the amendment to the Constitution, Carrie again spoke for the nation's women. "We are no longer petitioners, we are not wards of the nation but free and equal citizens."

With No sacredness of the ballot there can be no SACREDNESS of human life itself.

The MEMPHIS FREE SPEECH AND HEADLIGHT

14

Ida B. Wells-Barnett

JULY 16, 1862–MARCH 25, 1931

THE WAY TO RIGHT WRONGS IS TO TURN THE LIGHT OF TRUTH UPON THEM.

IDA BELL WELLS had to grow up fast. At the age of sixteen, she and her five younger siblings were orphaned. Her father, mother, and baby brother died in a yellow fever epidemic that raged through Holly Springs, Mississippi, in 1878.

Ida had been born a slave. Her father was of mixed ancestry—his mother was a slave and his father was her white owner. Her mother was part African American, part Native American. But when Ida was six months old, she and her family were freed by the Emancipation Proclamation.

Her mother became a cook and her father was a carpenter who helped start a university for freed slaves. It was while she was a student at the college that Ida's parents died. "After being a light-hearted school girl, I suddenly found myself at the head of a family," she said.

Without consulting Ida, family friends decided to divide the children among different homes and send Ida's disabled sister to an institution. But Ida had other ideas.

She convinced a school six miles out of town that she was eighteen and could teach. It was a hard life—she commuted by mule—but she kept her family together for two years. Tragedy struck again when her grandmother, who helped with childcare, had a stroke, and Ida and her sisters went to live with an aunt in Memphis.

In Memphis, Ida encountered real racism. One day in 1884, she boarded a train to Nashville, Tennessee. At only five feet tall, she was a tiny woman. She was dressed fashionably in a full-length corseted dress, a hat, and gloves. She carried an overnight

What was with suffragists and their parades? These days, you might go to the Macy's Thanksgiving Day parade or a Memorial Day parade, but parades are not as popular an entertainment as they used to be.

Here's the thing. In earlier eras, well-bred women never—ever!—set foot in the street, and they rarely walked anywhere in public without a male escorting them. "To a woman brought up as I was, it was a terrible ordeal," said socialite and suffragist Alva Vanderbilt Belmont after she had marched. On October 23, 1915, Katrina Ely Tiffany was among twenty-five thousand women who paraded down New York's Fifth Avenue. Her husband, Charles L. Tiffany II, watched in horror from the windows of their famous jewelry store.

But parading in the street created just the kind of stir suffragists wanted. They made their parades into pageants, complete with floats, bands, and staged scenes depicting liberty, freedom, and justice. Crowds often turned ugly, but no matter how humiliating or how dangerous the parade, the women kept walking.

bag and a parasol. She had a thirty-five-cent ticket for the first-class ladies' car, and she settled into her seat. But the railroad had segregated cars, and the conductor insisted she ride in the "colored car" at the back of the train.

Ida refused.

The conductor and several passengers dragged Ida kicking and screaming down the aisle. Pulling at her arm, the conductor tore a sleeve off her dress. "The moment he caught hold of my arm I fastened my teeth in the back of his hand," she said. Still, they managed to haul her off the train. But Ida didn't back down—she sued the railroad and won!

Ida's life of activism started on that train. She began writing articles about the treatment of African Americans for local newspapers. While still holding down a teaching job, she became a contributor to *The Evening Star*, a black-owned newspaper in Washington, DC. Nothing could have suited her better. "It was through journalism that I found the real me," she said.

Through her reporting, Ida began battling racial injustices, such as the poor condition of black schools and Jim Crow segregation laws in the South. For Ida, there was only one way to erase bias: "The way to right wrongs is to turn the light of truth upon them."

In 1888, as the editor and co-owner of *The Memphis Free Speech and Headlight*, she zeroed in on the injustice that most outraged her—lynching. At a lynching, racist mobs kidnapped, tortured, and shot or hanged African Americans, often in front of jeering crowds. Three friends of Ida's had been brutally lynched after defending their grocery store from a mob of white men.

Ida's protest on the train in Memphis, Tennessee, took place seventy-one years before Rosa Parks refused to give her seat on a bus to a white person in Montgomery, Alabama.

Her outspokenness in Memphis put her life in danger. She received death threats and was stalked on her way to and from work. In 1892, a gang of white men burned down the office of the *Memphis Free Speech*. It was time for Ida to leave—she first moved to New York and the next year to Chicago.

There, she continued to write, and in 1895, married attorney Ferdinand Barnett. The couple had four children, but her busy home life didn't keep Ida from her activism—she added suffrage to her crusade against lynching. In 1913, Illinois granted women the right to vote in national elections. But, seeing that African American women in Chicago weren't becoming involved in the national suffrage fight, she founded the Alpha Suffrage Club, the first black women's suffrage association.

On March 3, 1913, suffragists staged a massive parade in Washington, DC, and women poured in from around the country. The Alpha Suffrage Club sent a delegation. Shockingly, organizers told Ida that black women had to march at the back of the parade. They worried that their cause would be hurt if people saw black and white women walking together. They thought lawmakers would resist suffrage if it meant boundaries separating the races would be erased.

When the parade began, Ida was nowhere to be found. Her friends and colleagues wondered whether she'd gone home. But as the women paraded down the street, Ida popped out from the crowd of onlookers. Calmly, she fell in line with the white Illinois delegation. No one dared drag her away this time.

After the governor of Illinois signed the bill granting women in Ida's adopted state the right to vote, suffrage leader Carrie Chapman Catt said that "suffrage sentiment doubled overnight." National suffrage was still seven years away, but through her activism, Ida had moved the needle.

A Colored Woman in A White World

When the WORLD takes a STEP forward in PROGRESS, some OLD custom falls Dead at OUR feet.

15

Mary Church Terrell

SEPTEMBER 23, 1863–JULY 24, 1954

LIFTING AS WE CLIMB, ONWARD AND UPWARD WE GO.

MARY CHURCH had never given her skin color a thought. She knew her parents were both former slaves, but she didn't realize that other people might look at her differently because of that.

Until one day at school.

From the age of eight years old, Mary attended a boarding school in Ohio that enrolled both white and African American children. One day, she came on a group of white girls who were bragging about their looks. One was proud of her hair, another the shape of her mouth, yet another the color of her eyes. Joining in the fun, Mary asked, "Haven't I got a pretty face, too?"

"You've got a pretty *black* face," one of the girls said, pointing at Mary and laughing. All the other girls laughed, too. "For the first time in my life I realized that I was an object of ridicule on account of the color of my skin," she said.

Mary used that hurt to guide her path as an adult. She had an unusual childhood for an African American girl in the South. Her father, the son of a slave and her white owner, was a freed slave. Settling in Memphis, he became a millionaire by buying a tavern and, with the profits, buying up more real estate. Much of his wealth came from buying property that was abandoned during the yellow fever outbreaks of the late 1870s. Her mother had her own business—a rare thing for a woman of any race at the time. She owned a hair salon that catered to society women.

Even after her parents divorced, Mary never wanted for anything. She attended private schools and Oberlin College—she was one of the first African American

> Mary learned three languages besides English— German, French, and Italian. When she lectured overseas, audiences adored her because she could speak to many of them in their own language.

women to graduate from college. She had silk dresses, a generous allowance, and took frequent vacations—she even went on a two-year European tour. She had a marriage proposal from a German baron. In 1881, she attended President James Garfield's inaugural ball as the guest of Senator Blanche Bruce, the second African American to be elected to the U.S. Senate.

But all the while, she felt the pain of African Americans whose lives were nearly as bad as their lives in slavery. She believed that education and hard work could change things. After college, she taught at a high school for black children in Washington, DC, where she met her husband, Robert Terrell, a Harvard-educated lawyer and later the first African American man to be named a municipal court judge.

When she married, Mary was forced to stop teaching, so she threw her energies into reform causes. She helped found organizations that worked for better education, jobs, healthcare, and living conditions for African Americans—the Colored Woman's League of Washington, the National Association of Colored Women, the National Association for the Advancement of Colored People, and the College Alumnae Club, among others. During one twelve-year period, Mary was involved in twenty-nine different clubs.

Suffrage was a natural concern for Mary. She met Susan B. Anthony in 1898 and began working to gain the vote for women. She was vocal about the double blow dealt African American women. "The word 'people' has been turned and twisted to mean all who were shrewd and wise enough to have themselves born boys instead of girls, or who took the trouble to be born white instead of black," she noted wryly.

Mary frequently spoke in the South, where suffrage for African American women faced fierce opposition. She was forced to ride in segregated train cars, barred from restaurants, refused hotel rooms. She feared for her life, yet she carried on. "It gives me satisfaction to know that I was on the right side of the question when it was most unpopular to advocate it," she said. Even in the North, Mary faced prejudice. In 1911, lawyers prevented black and white suffragists from meeting together to hear Mary speak in the Manhattan home of social and educational reformer John Dewey.

Mary was a leader within the black women's suffrage movement at a time when most white suffragists weren't willing to work with African American women. But she also managed to work within white suffragist groups, bringing African American women into the wider fight. She spoke on behalf of the National American Woman Suffrage Association and picketed the White House with the radical suffragists of the National Woman's Party. "Graceful, eloquent, logical—Mrs. Terrell is one of the coming women of America," said Isabella Beecher Hooker.

For her entire life, Mary worked to improve the "crushed and blighted lives" of her people. She not only lived to see women get the vote but later became a pioneer of the modern civil rights movement. In the 1950s, when she was in her eighties, she led protests against department store restaurants that barred African Americans. "And so, lifting as we climb, onward and upward we go, struggling and striving," she'd say. "Seeking no favors because of our color, nor patronage because of our needs, we knock at the bar of justice, asking an equal chance."

Early leaders of the suffrage movement looked pretty much alike—women who were white and wealthy. But the battle was won only after the movement was opened up to others.

Mary worked tirelessly for African American suffrage and women's groups, as did Mary Ann Shadd Cary and Ida B. Wells-Barnett. It was primarily through these groups that African Americans were introduced to the suffrage campaign.

"Whatever is unusual is called unnatural the world over," she'd say about the vote. "When the world takes a step forward in progress, some old custom falls dead at our feet."

Harriot Stanton Blatch, the daughter of Elizabeth Cady Stanton, saw the future of suffrage in working women. In 1907, she formed the Equality League of Self-Supporting Women. "It was gradually borne in upon us that the enthusiasm in the suffrage movement in the future would come from the industrial women," she said.

New to the job force, women were not being protected by labor laws. This became tragically clear on March 25, 1911, when 146 workers at the Triangle Shirtwaist Factory in New York City died in a fire. The owners had locked the exits to keep workers—almost all women—from taking breaks. Harriot Blatch thought the woman's vote could reform cruel labor practices like these.

16

Lucy Burns

JULY 28, 1879–DECEMBER 22, 1966

MR. PRESIDENT, WHAT WILL YOU DO FOR WOMAN SUFFRAGE?

PERCHED ON a pool table in a London police station, Lucy Burns chatted away with Alice Paul, the only other American who had been arrested that day.

The two women had been protesting with British suffragists outside of Parliament. The date was June 29, 1909. It was Lucy's first arrest—she had slapped a policeman and wrested his whistle away from him. At the police station, Alice introduced herself after noticing the American flag pin on Lucy's coat. The two elbowed their way through the crowd of a hundred women to the only place they could find to sit.

From that day on, the names of these two women would be forever linked.

Little is known about Lucy's childhood. She was born in the Park Slope neighborhood of Brooklyn to Irish-American parents. She was an avid learner—her studies took her to Vassar, Yale, Columbia, Oxford, and two universities in Germany. She seized opportunities that women before her had been denied.

Lucy was at Oxford, but tiring of her endless studies, when she went to her first suffrage meeting. The speaker, Emmeline Pankhurst, was electrifying. She led British suffragists into militant activism, disrupting political meetings, setting fires on golf courses, and hurling rocks through windows.

Lucy admired the British suffragists. "I was very much impressed by their moral ardor, optimism and buoyancy of spirit," she said. She dove headfirst into the fight.

Lucy threw ink bottles and broke police station windows. She was arrested and sent to prison three times and went on hunger strikes twice. "We sleepy Americans don't know what a go-ahead country this is," she wrote to her friends. Lucy was a striking presence in suffrage circles, her flaming red hair piled dramatically on top of her head and her blue eyes blazing with passion.

"Deeds, not words" was the motto of the British suffragists Lucy so admired. By that phrase, they meant that lawmakers should stop talking and start taking action. American suffragists took another famous slogan—"Votes for Women!"—from their British sisters.

In 1912, Lucy brought her activism home. She and Alice started a committee of the National American Woman Suffrage Association in Washington, DC. Lucy was quickly arrested for chalking a suffrage message on a sidewalk. She paid the one dollar fine, but she was just getting started.

Lucy organized a tour through the West to convince voters to defeat anti-suffrage candidates. At first, NAWSA welcomed Alice and Lucy. But soon, the pair became too radical for the staid organization, and they split off to form their own organization, the Congressional Union for Woman Suffrage.

The next year, on March 3, 1913, they organized a suffrage parade in Washington, DC, stealing President Woodrow Wilson's thunder on his inauguration weekend. Mobs of drunken men harassed the eight thousand women as they fought their way up Pennsylvania Avenue. Men jeered, spat at the women, tripped them, tore their clothing, beat them with the poles of their banners, and stubbed out cigars on their arms. Police stood idly by. Three hundred women were treated for injuries.

Three years later, on December 5, 1916, Lucy and nine other women attended Wilson's annual address to Congress. They unfurled a banner from the visitors' gallery that read, "Mr. President, What Will You Do for Woman Suffrage?" Men below hoisted a young boy on their shoulders, and he ripped the banner from their hands while security guards surrounded the women.

Becoming impatient, the women began a series of pickets outside the White House in January 1917. Police were increasingly rough with the "Silent Sentinels" who stood outside in all weather holding suffrage banners aloft. Eventually, they started arresting and jailing them. Lucy was the first picketer to be arrested, and she spent more time in prison than any other suffragist.

One day in April 1917, at the height of World War I, picketers unfurled banners calling the president "Kaiser Wilson," likening him to Germany's Kaiser Wilhelm II, whom the United States was fighting. The patriotic crowd was outraged. They chased picketers back to the group's headquarters, where soldiers tried to throw Lucy over a second-story balcony. She dangled briefly over the railing while people below gasped. Someone in the crowd fired a shot through a second-story window, narrowly missing several women inside.

On November 14, 1917, Lucy was again arrested. In what came to be known as the Night of Terror, the suffragists were taken to Occoquan Workhouse in Lorton, Virginia.

Guards dragged the women to the cells and threw them like rag dolls on the floor and against iron benches and beds. They were denied food and water and left bruised and battered.

In the ensuing prison stint, Lucy started a hunger strike, seeking to force officials to grant the suffragists the status of political prisoners, not criminals. After a week, she was brutally force fed, as she had been in England. "I was held down by five people.... I refused to open mouth. [Doctor] pushed tube up left nostril...it makes nose bleed freely," she wrote on a scrap of paper smuggled out of prison.

Even prison terms and hunger strikes didn't deter Lucy. She organized watchfires in a park across from the White House, where protestors fed copies of Wilson's wartime speeches on democracy into the flames. Having been denied the full rights of citizenship, they found the president's words laughable. Brazenly, they even burned an effigy of the president. And they continued to go to prison—Lucy was jailed six times altogether. "She was a thousand times more valiant than I," Alice Paul said of her.

Day after day, under Lucy's leadership, the women kept up their pressure. Yet when suffrage finally came in 1920, Lucy was physically and emotionally broken and ready to pass the baton to the next generation. "We have sacrificed everything we possessed for them.... Now let them fight for it," she said. She retired from public view, and after her sister died in childbirth, devoted herself to raising her niece. The rebel who had upped the ante in the suffrage battle took her fighting spirit home.

The Night of Terror—

November 14–15, 1917—changed public opinion about the suffragists forever.

That night, police hauled thirty-one picketers off to Occoquan Workhouse. They were beaten with fists and clubs as they went and were dragged down into dark, filthy, and airless cells. One woman blacked out when guards threw her against an iron bed. Another woman suffered a heart attack. Knowing Lucy to be the leader, guards shackled her hands over her head to the cell door, where she remained all night. When she refused to put on prison clothes the next day, they stripped her and gave her only a thin, dirty blanket to cover herself.

Serving prison terms that were handed down after that night, the suffragists shivered with the cold. Rodents and cockroaches ran over them as they lay on bug-infested mats. Open toilets fouled the air. They were fed worm-ridden slop and worked in sweatshop conditions. Lucy started yet another hunger strike, along with more than two dozen other prisoners. She turned away when guards tried to tempt her with a chicken dinner. "They think there is nothing in our souls above fried chicken," she scoffed. When people learned of their treatment—and of the horrors of force feeding—public opinion turned in favor of the suffragists.

I may be the FIRST Woman member of CONGRESS, but I won't be the LAST.

VOTES FOR WOMEN

17

Jeannette Rankin

JUNE 11, 1880-MAY 18, 1973

HOW SHALL WE ANSWER THEIR CHALLENGE, GENTLEMEN?

JEANNETTE RANKIN liked to make hats. Big, dramatic hats trimmed with ribbons and flowers and swooping plumes of feathers. Little did she know that one day she would wear a hugely symbolic, history-making hat—that of the first woman elected to Congress.

Jeannette was born in Montana before it was a state. It was a wild, rugged territory that had long been home to Native Americans and, more recently, fur trappers, gold miners, and cattle ranchers. Her family had a ranch outside Missoula, where Jeannette spent most of her childhood.

Jeannette helped her mother with family chores. She cooked at her father's lumber camp and helped run his hotel. She took care of her five siblings. But she was bossy, and when she didn't get her way, she threw tantrums. One day, her mother said to Jeannette's father, "If you can take care of Jeannette, I can take care of the rest of the children."

To be fair to Jeannette, no one in the family was a shrinking violet. They loved to argue, and when tempers flared, they were known to throw dishes, silverware, and glasses of water at each other.

Jeannette rode horses across the windswept plains and into mountain canyons. The classroom couldn't contain her. "I was a very poor student and I didn't enjoy going to school," she admitted.

In the West, newly arrived settlers were driving Native Americans from their ancestral lands. Jeannette's father was angry about their cruel treatment. He argued that war solved nothing—it just led to more bloodshed. Jeannette absorbed his opinions.

All the while, Jeannette was impatient with her domestic life. "Go! Go! Go! At the first opportunity go!" she urged herself in her diary.

After getting her degree from Montana State University in 1902, Jeannette took the familiar path of teaching, but she became bored. For a change, she took a job with a milliner, a person who makes hats. Making hats really brought out Jeannette's creative side! She looked regal, with her confident manner and outrageous, wide-brimmed hats.

In 1907, at the age of twenty-seven, Jeannette moved to San Francisco to take a job in social work. Later, she enrolled in a social worker's course in New York City, where she was horrified by the conditions in urban slums. She then moved to Spokane, Washington, to continue her career in social work.

Again on the move, Jeannette went to Seattle for further studies. It was in Seattle that Jeannette found her true cause. While there, she spotted a poster seeking volunteers for suffrage work. In 1910, she began working for the vote in Washington State.

Hattie Wyatt Caraway of Arkansas was the first woman elected to the U.S. Senate. She was appointed to her husband's seat when he died in office in 1931, but then won election to the seat in 1932 and again in 1938.

When she returned to Montana in 1911, Jeannette pressed for reforms in Missoula's judicial and prison systems, and she was relentless. "My God, that woman again!" one judge cried when he saw her coming. At the same time, she started organizing local suffrage groups.

On February 1, 1911, Jeannette became the first person to address Montana's state lawmakers about suffrage. Her success at grassroots organizing attracted the attention of Carrie Chapman Catt, and soon she was working at the national level.

Jeannette's passion did cause trouble at times. One night at a suffrage office, she lost her temper and began throwing things. A friend gently led her away and later scolded her. "Once in a while I want to spank you good and hard," she wrote to Jeannette. "Now, will you be good?"

Montana granted women the right to vote in 1914, and Jeannette had an idea. *What if I run for Congress?* Montana had two seats in the House of Representatives, so she could win an election even if she came in second. Her brother, a powerful lawyer, agreed to help run her campaign.

Jeannette put her skill at campaigning and grassroots organizing to work again. On November 6, 1916, Jeannette voted for the first time—for herself! The next morning, the results were tallied, and Jeannette had won the second seat.

On April 2, 1917, suffragists honored her at a special breakfast in Washington, DC. Jeannette swept into Congress that day cradling a bouquet of purple and yellow flowers—the colors of the radical suffragists. Her colleagues and the crowd of suffrage supporters in the galleries rose and applauded her wholeheartedly.

That day, President Woodrow Wilson called on Congress to vote for war against Germany. Along with forty-nine men, Jeannette voted against war. She firmly believed—despite her epic outbursts—that violence solved nothing.

Even so, Jeannette was always up for the suffrage fight. "How shall we answer their challenge, gentlemen?" she asked her fellow lawmakers. "How shall we explain to them the meaning of democracy if the same Congress that voted to make the world safe for democracy refuses to give this small measure of democracy to the women of our country?"

By the time she left office in March 1919, Congress was just months away from passing the Nineteenth Amendment. Denying women the vote no longer made sense when one of their number was sitting in a congressional seat.

Western states were more open to the idea of woman suffrage than eastern states. Why was that?

Women in many western states could vote for president long before the Nineteenth Amendment was enacted. In 1869, when it was still a territory, Wyoming granted women the vote. When it became a state in 1890, it entered the Union as the first state in which women could vote. Colorado, Utah, Idaho, Washington, California, Arizona—one by one, western states gave women the vote.

These states might have wanted to attract more women, believing they would improve the moral tone of their rough-and-tumble frontier towns. Or, it might be that women had already proved their worth there, working just as hard as men to settle the West. Perhaps at times politics had something to do with it. One story goes that the ailing wife of a politician in one western state was treated by a local doctor, and in gratitude, the politician asked what favor he could do for the doctor. The doctor's wife had the answer—she wanted the vote!

Old Spain in our Southwest

I will take a STAND and a firm one whenever NECESSARY.

Adelina Otero-Warren

OCTOBER 23, 1881–JANUARY 23, 1965

WE WILL WIN.

MARIA ADELINA ISABEL EMILIA OTERO—Nina, for short—was born into an Hispano family that enjoyed wealth and status in the sprawling territory of New Mexico.

Nina's father, Manuel Otero, came from a noble Spanish family. Her mother, Eloisa Luna, was descended from people who came to the New World with Spanish conquistadors like Cortés and Coronado—one of her ancestors was even a pope of the Catholic Church in the 1300s. Nina was born into a world of social standing and political power.

The Oteros held vast acres of land south of Albuquerque, on which they raised sheep and grew crops. They made a fortune in the California gold rush, when they drove twenty-five thousand head of sheep from their ranch to the booming state and sold them at top dollar.

Nina was a bold girl. She rode horses with her brothers, overseeing the ranch and its workers. She insisted they teach her how to shoot a pistol. But her family saw to it that she also got a fine education, attending a Catholic boarding school in Kansas City until the age of thirteen.

Returning to New Mexico, she was tasked with teaching her nine younger siblings. Nina's father had died when she was a baby, gunned down in a dispute with two white men over land, and her mother's remarriage had created a large, blended family. Nina enjoyed her role as a teacher.

The family moved to Santa Fe in 1897, when a cousin was appointed governor of the territory. Nina thrived in her new surroundings. She had a mane of thick red hair

In Nina's part of the country, girls could marry at age fifteen. But Nina wasn't interested in marriage at that age.

She was twenty-six years old when she married Rawson Warren, an army officer. As an Hispano woman married to an Anglo man, she was the subject of gossip and disapproval. Moving around to far-flung military bases, she was torn from her large and loving family. Within two years, Nina divorced Warren. At the time, not only was divorce frowned on in general, but New Mexico was a largely Catholic state where divorce carried an even greater stigma. It's no wonder she chose to let people think she was widowed.

In the 1930s, Nina and her close friend and colleague Mamie Meadors bought a homestead of more than twelve hundred acres a few miles northwest of Santa Fe, on which they built two homes. They spent long stretches of time there for many years. In the 1940s, the two women went into business together, starting an insurance and real estate agency called Las Dos, meaning The Two. They worked together until Mamie's death in 1951.

and hazel eyes that flashed with intelligence and humor. She was admired for her charm and wit, and friends called her "high spirited and independent." Her family moved in the powerful political circles of the boomtown.

In the culture of the western United States, women often had more rights and opportunities than their eastern sisters, even in traditionally male-dominated Hispanic communities. Nina's mother brought land and money into her marriage, and she passed it on to her daughters at her death. She was also the first female member of the Santa Fe school board. Nina always assumed she would live a life of influence.

But when New Mexico became a state in 1912, its constitution denied women the right to vote. Angered, Nina took up suffrage in earnest. In her state, there was no organized support for the cause until Alice Paul, cofounder of the National Woman's Party, tapped Nina to head the state's suffrage campaign. "I am with you now and always!" Nina wrote to Alice.

Nina came up against the same male scorn that plagued her eastern colleagues. Women who wanted the vote were willing to "trade their good looks for a cheap fame," scoffed one of Nina's brothers-in-law. Although Hispanic culture granted women some respect, at its heart it was still a man's world.

Nina and the New Mexico suffragists suffered setback after setback, until February 1920, when the state finally voted on the Nineteenth Amendment. "Situation in Senate favorable . . . Fight on in House . . . But we will win," she wrote in a telegram to Alice Paul. And thanks to Nina's leadership and political clout, New Mexico became the thirty-second state to ratify the Nineteenth Amendment.

Nina moved easily between different worlds—Hispanic and Anglo, male and female. She was from an upper-class family, yet she worked for the welfare of people from all stations in life. She was single and childless, yet made a career in the education of children. In 1917, she was elected by an all-male board as superintendent of public schools in Santa Fe. She served as an officer of the Red Cross, a member of Santa Fe's board of health and public safety, and was chair of the women's division of the state Republican party.

Nina was afraid that Hispanic culture, with its unique arts, crafts, language, and traditions, would be crushed by Anglo culture. She worked tirelessly within schools and cultural institutions to make sure that didn't happen. Her book, *Old Spain in Our Southwest*, contains stories of the daily life, history, songs, and myths of this culture.

Despite her many successes, Nina was denied the groundbreaking role she sought after women gained the vote. In 1922, Nina won her state's Republican nomination for a seat in the U.S. House of Representatives. She was the first Hispanic woman to run for national office. She was defeated when a male relative revealed that Nina had divorced her husband but passed herself off as a widow. Nina lost the election and never again ran for public office. But through her activism, she emboldened the women of New Mexico to claim a place in the political realm.

It is worth sacrificing EVERYTHING for—leisure, money, Reputation, and even our LIVES.

19

Alice Paul

JANUARY 11, 1885–JULY 9, 1977

VOTES FOR WOMEN!

PICTURE THIS: A young Quaker girl on the lawn of her family's gracious home in the country. She's playing tennis with her sister and brothers. Or, she's playing checkers on the wraparound porch. Maybe she's in the library, absorbed in the novels of Charles Dickens. She's a quiet, obedient, nice little girl.

Now picture this little girl as a young woman in the bustling Scottish city of Edinburgh. Her wrists are handcuffed behind her back and policemen are parading her through the streets. She's scaling a government building in Glasgow, lying on the roof at night in a pouring rain, waiting to break through in the morning to disrupt a political meeting. She's in a London prison, held down by five people, thrashing about wildly as she tries to escape the feeding tube the prison doctor is jamming down her throat. She's a forceful, determined, angry young woman.

Alice Paul was both the quiet Quaker girl and the militant suffragist.

Alice's background hardly hinted at the woman she would become. She grew up in New Jersey in an eighth-generation Quaker family and absorbed its sober, peaceful ways. She was sheltered from the outside world. "I never met anybody who wasn't a Quaker, except that the maids we had were always Irish Catholics," she said.

Alice's mother was curious about suffrage, and she took Alice along with her to suffrage meetings at friends' houses. The ideas Alice heard stayed with her when she went off in 1901 to Swarthmore, a college her grandfather had helped found, and then to do social work in New York City after she graduated in 1905.

Pretty quickly, Alice realized that social work wasn't for her. She didn't see her efforts changing the conditions that poor people endured. In 1907, she went to the University of Pennsylvania for graduate studies and then to England for more studies. While there, she attended a lecture by Christabel Pankhurst, the daughter of British

The fight for the woman's vote didn't really start in 1848 with the Declaration of Sentiments. Suffragist ideas reached back much further in our nation's history.

During the Second Continental Congress that met in 1776 to form a national government, Abigail Adams urged her husband, future president John Adams, to "remember the ladies." "If particular care and attention is not paid to the ladies," she warned, "we are determined to foment a rebellion and will not hold ourselves bound by any laws in which we have no voice or representation."

And, although America had broken away from the British crown, American suffragists considered Englishwoman Mary Wollstonecraft to be a mentor. (You might have heard of her daughter, Mary Shelley—the author of *Frankenstein*.) In her 1792 book, *A Vindication of the Rights of Woman*, Wollstonecraft argued that women's lowly status was due to a lack of education, not a lack of intelligence or ability. "Truth must be common to all," she wrote.

Early in the 1800s, the American writer Margaret Fuller talked about expanding women's role in society. Her 1845 book, *Woman in the Nineteenth Century*, made a case for political equality and a larger, more public life for women. "She possessed more influence on the thought of American women than any woman previous to her time," said founders of the suffrage movement.

suffrage leader Emmeline Pankhurst. The crowd heckled her, drowning out her words, but Alice was hooked.

In one of Alice's first militant acts, she and her friend Amelia Brown sneaked into a political banquet in 1909 dressed as maids, complete with mops and brooms. From a balcony overlooking the main floor, Amelia smashed a window with her shoe and the two cried out, "Votes for women!"

That same year, Alice was arrested at a Parliament protest and ended up at the police station where she met Lucy Burns. The two formed a fierce alliance, just as Elizabeth Cady Stanton and Susan B. Anthony had done a generation earlier.

Alice was jailed three times in England. It was there that she first went on hunger strikes and endured the nightmare of force feeding. Twice a day, guards held her down and a doctor forced a rigid, unwashed feeding tube down her throat or nose. The ice-cold milk and raw eggs they dumped in made her sick to her stomach, and she would vomit it all back up again. In college, Alice had been a small but hearty girl, active in sports. By the time she came back to the United States in 1910, she was thin, pale, and frail-looking.

At home, the suffragist cause was sputtering. At first, the National American Woman Suffrage Association appreciated Alice and Lucy for their youth and enthusiasm. But soon, they ran afoul of the women who practiced polite, respectful lobbying. Alice and Lucy wanted the kind of action they had seen in England, and so they split off on their own, forming the Congressional Union.

In Washington, DC, Alice organized parades and protests and rallied women from around the country. But she, too, could be prejudiced. In the massive suffrage parade of 1913, it was she who ordered black delegates, including Ida B. Wells-Barnett, to march separately at the back of the parade. Ida and other black women defied Alice's misguided attempt to gain the public's support through an act of racism.

Alice Paul wrote the Equal Rights Amendment in 1923. Called the Lucretia Mott Amendment, it addressed inequalities, such as lower pay, that women face. It was finally approved by Congress in 1972, but didn't win enough states to be ratified.

Despite the growing influence of the suffragists, Congress and the president continued to ignore their protests, so Alice doubled down. She started a political party, the National Woman's Party, and organized pickets to demonstrate outside the White House gates. Suffragists could boast a notable civil rights first—they were the first organized group to picket the White House.

After organizing the first protest on January 10, 1917, Alice got a letter at the party's offices. "Dear Alice, I wish to make a protest against the methods you are adopting in annoying the President. . . . I hope thee will call it off." The letter was from her mother!

Alice didn't call it off. Instead, she was jailed three more times, in vile prisons overseen by cruel wardens. Again, she joined hunger strikes, even though she knew the brutality of force feeding. Alice's agonized screams echoed throughout the prison. "Don't let them tell you we take this well," a fellow prisoner said. "Miss Paul vomits much . . . it is horrible."

Prison officials went so far as to try to commit Alice to an insane asylum. And, at times, she had to be hospitalized. But still she fought. "It is worth sacrificing everything for—leisure, money, reputation and even our lives," she insisted.

When suffrage was granted in 1920, Alice celebrated quietly by unfurling a banner displaying thirty-six stars from the balcony of her headquarters—one for each state that ratified the amendment. Carrie Chapman Catt got President Wilson's congratulations and a victory parade in New York City, but Alice's activism didn't go unnoticed. "Your place in history is assured. . . . It is certain that, but for you, success would have been delayed for many years to come," one well-wisher told her.

Even Alice's gentle, worried mother applauded her daughter's success. "Suffrage was granted to women & we voted for the first time for the President Nov. 1920," she wrote in her diary. "Alice at last saw her dream realized."

Indeed she did. Alice and the long line of passionate suffragists who came before her.

20

And Don't Forget

HISTORIC FIGURES like those in this book became famous for their activism. Countless others who fought for the cause are nameless today, coming down to us at most as faces in old black-and-white photographs.

Some suffragists are known for a single act or a single moment in their lives. Or, they may have contributed significantly to women's rights, but they've been overlooked due to prejudice. Others are major historical figures whose well-known accomplishments have overshadowed their suffrage activism. If we take just a moment to consider their lives, their bold actions can speak to us today, encouraging us to act on our own strongly held beliefs.

PARKER PILLSBURY » September 22, 1809–July 7, 1898

It took a brave man to back the unpopular woman's cause. Parker was that man. He was ahead of his time in seeking the ballot for all. "It is mockery to talk of liberty and the pursuit of happiness, until the ballot in the hand of every citizen seals and secures it," he said. In 1865, he helped draft the founding document of the American Equal Rights Association.

Parker believed that men should use systems over which they had control—like the vote—to empower women. Men claimed they were being gallant by shielding women from the nasty world of politics, but Parker didn't buy it. He urged men to tame their desire to bully women, even by seeming to protect them.

Parker's commitment to his causes was costly. He lost his job as a minister and he barely scraped by. His health suffered and he was absent from his family much of the time. But Parker was so valuable to the suffrage cause that Susan B. Anthony and Elizabeth Cady Stanton chose him as coeditor of their influential women's rights newspaper, *The Revolution*.

FREDERICK DOUGLASS » c. February 1818–February 20, 1895

Frederick understood what it was like to be at the mercy of others. He was brutally and cruelly enslaved until he escaped at the age of twenty. He could see that without the vote women suffered from their own kind of slavery. "She is absolutely in the hands of her political masters," he said.

Frederick attended the Seneca Falls convention, where he was the only man invited to speak. He was one of sixty-eight women and thirty-two men to sign the Declaration of Sentiments, and he became a forceful speaker in favor of the woman's ballot. Even when friendships frayed over the question of whether African American men should get the vote before women did, he never deserted the woman's cause.

It is only because of Frederick Douglass that we know exactly what the Declaration of Sentiments said. He published it word for word in his Rochester, New York, newspaper, *The North Star*. The original has never turned up anywhere. It may have been destroyed when his house burned down in 1872.

AMELIA JENKS BLOOMER » May 27, 1818–December 30, 1894

Women's clothing in the 1800s was hot and heavy. A simple walk was almost impossible. Even at the beach, a woman had to wear ankle-length skirts and knit stockings.

Amelia popularized a clothing style of loose pants topped by a tunic that became known as the "bloomer costume." Many suffragists adopted the style, delighted by its comfort and practicality. Yet it quickly fell out of favor because both men and women made fun of the new look. Afraid that their dress would hurt the suffrage cause, women went back to their constricting clothes—at least in public.

Amelia made a more lasting contribution to suffrage by introducing Elizabeth Cady Stanton to Susan B. Anthony. She was also the first woman to start a newspaper that addressed women's issues. She founded *The Lily* a year after the 1848 Seneca Falls convention. The bloomer costume first appeared in her paper.

VICTORIA WOODHULL » September 23, 1838–June 9, 1927

Victoria grew up with a violent, alcoholic con man father and a mother who thought herself a mystic. Her father burned down his gristmill in an illegal attempt to get insurance money, and he was run out of town, leaving Victoria and her mother to support themselves. From a young age, Victoria claimed to be a psychic who could talk with the dead—for a fee, of course.

Victoria led a free-spirited life that shocked people. She married three times and divorced twice. In 1870, she and her sister, with the backing of the wealthy tycoon Cornelius Vanderbilt, started the first female-led stock brokerage firm on Wall Street. She stirred up a national scandal in *Woodhull & Claflin's Weekly*, the newspaper she and her sister had founded, by publicly accusing a famous preacher—Isabella Beecher Hooker's brother—of having an affair. Her enemies called her "Mrs. Satan."

In 1871, Victoria became the first woman to address women's suffrage before a committee of the House of Representatives. The next year, she started her own political party, the Equal Rights Party, and declared herself a candidate for president, decades before women even had the right to vote.

JOSEPHINE ST. PIERRE RUFFIN » August 31, 1842–March 13, 1924

Josephine's mother was an Englishwoman and her father was from the West Indian island of Martinique. She went to a rare school in Salem, Massachusetts, that taught children of all ethnicities side by side.

She was a founding member of the Massachusetts Woman Suffrage Association, along with Julia Ward Howe and Lucy Stone. In 1895, she also founded the first national club for black women, the Women's Era. She edited the club's monthly newspaper, voicing opinions about suffrage and the ill treatment of African American people. The motto of the club and its newspaper was "Aim to Make the World Better"—words spoken by Lucy Stone on her deathbed.

Josephine wanted all women's clubs to work together to gain the reforms everyone wanted. But prejudice was slow to die. In 1900, she tried to convince the General Federation of Women's Clubs to admit the Women's Era club, but she was defeated by votes from southern states.

NINA EVANS ALLENDER » December 25, 1873–April 2, 1957

Writing and speaking weren't the only talents women brought to the suffrage fight. Artists like Nina drew attention to the cause with vivid, memorable images.

Nina's cartoons were featured in *The Suffragist*, the newspaper of the National Woman's Party. Women identified with the new "Suffrage Girl," a bold and confident, but entirely feminine, American woman. Until Nina came along, male cartoonists depicted suffragists as ugly, strident hags.

Alice Paul asked Nina to design the famous "Jailed for Freedom" suffrage pin. Each of the 168 women jailed for picketing the White House was awarded one of these silver pins. It depicts a prison cell door secured with a heart-shaped lock and chain. In February 1919, in what was called the Prison Special, the jailed—but now decorated—suffragists began touring the country by train, speaking about their ordeal to rally public support for passage of the Nineteenth Amendment.

INEZ MILHOLLAND BOISSEVAIN » August 6, 1886–November 25, 1916

As a student at Vassar, Inez ignored an order from the college president not to promote suffrage. One day, she led a group of almost fifty female students to a nearby cemetery. Four suffragists, including Harriot Stanton Blatch, met them there. She unfurled a banner that read, "Come, let us reason together." She had started a suffrage club.

Inez led many of the suffrage parades, becoming the face of the movement with her commanding presence. In 1913, she was stationed at the head of the suffrage parade of eight thousand women in Washington, DC, astride a white horse. Wearing a white gown and flowing cape, with a tiara perched atop her mass of curls, she personified the ideal of the heroic suffragist.

Inez was also a lawyer who worked for a firm in New York City. In her professional and personal lives she championed many reform causes, including job opportunities and safe workplaces for women.

At the age of thirty, Inez became a martyr for the suffrage cause after she collapsed on stage giving a speech in Los Angeles. She died ten days later of pernicious anemia.

NELL RICHARDSON » 1890–?
AND ALICE SNITJER BURKE » May 12, 1875–February 11, 1948

By the early 1900s, cars had been invented and were gaining popularity, but women weren't considered fit to drive. Nell Richardson and Alice Burke disagreed! They seized the chance to promote suffrage with a road trip.

On April 6, 1916, they set off from New York City in a Saxon roadster on a ten-thousand-mile loop around the country. It was a difficult and dangerous journey—roads were rough, gas stations were few, and cars broke down frequently. They toted along everything they thought they'd need, from groceries and spare parts to evening gowns and a gun. They crossed deserts, got stuck in flooded rivers, and skirted the Mexican border as the U.S. Army fought the Mexican revolutionary Pancho Villa.

The women were on the road for almost five months. They took along a little black kitten named Saxon, who won the hearts of adoring crowds everywhere. Their car, painted in suffrage yellow and nicknamed the Golden Flier, became a beloved symbol of the movement.

HARRY T. BURN » November 12, 1895–February 19, 1977

Harry was only twenty-two years old when he was elected to the Tennessee General Assembly, yet his vote won ratification of the Nineteenth Amendment.

The amendment had passed in Congress in 1919, but it needed the approval of thirty-six states to become law. By August 1920, thirty-five states had signed on and the battle came to Tennessee. Would it become the thirty-sixth state, or would it kill the amendment? The State Senate passed the bill, but it looked like the House would be locked in a 48–48 tie.

Harry, who represented an anti-suffrage district in the House, had intended to vote "nay." But that morning he got a letter from his mother urging him to "be a good boy" and vote for woman suffrage. He did as he was told—his "aye" vote broke the tie. "I knew that a mother's advice is always safest for her boy to follow," he explained later.

CHARLOTTE WOODWARD PIERCE » 1829?–1921

In 1848, Charlotte was a teenaged glove maker who worked long hours for low pay. Even that little bit she had to turn over to her father. "Every fiber of my being rebelled," she said. She was intrigued when she saw the ad for the Seneca Falls convention.

Charlotte and a group of friends traveled forty miles in a horse-drawn wagon from her home in DeWitt, New York, to the convention. At the close of the convention, she signed the Declaration of Sentiments.

Throughout her life, Charlotte worked for the woman's vote, beginning with the American Woman Suffrage Association. In 1915, when she was eighty-six years old, she marched in the massive suffrage parade down New York's Fifth Avenue. And when the Nineteenth Amendment became law in 1920, Charlotte was the only signer of the Declaration of Sentiments still living. Yet when women voted for the first time in November, she was ninety-one years old and too ill to go to the polls. The widespread use of absentee ballots was more than ten years away.

Suffragists Julia Emory and Bertha Graf prepare to leave Washington, DC, on July 20, 1920, for a suffrage demonstration in Marion, Ohio, carrying bundles of rolled-up flags and banners.

Epilogue

A BATTLE UNTIL THE END

YOU WOULD LIKE to think that as the woman's suffrage fight neared the finish line, those who opposed it finally saw the light and readily agreed that the vote belonged to every citizen of the United States, male and female. But women had to fight for this right to the very end—and even after universal suffrage became law.

Despite decades of speech-making, traveling, writing, and petitioning, suffragists didn't have the satisfaction of seeing a constitutional amendment taken seriously until well into the 1900s. By the time Woodrow Wilson became president in 1913, they had begun to make headway with individual congressmen. But even after suffragists started picketing the White House during Wilson's second term, he paid little attention. When his driver took him through the gates, he would duck his head to avoid looking at the protesters.

Wilson was slow to back a federal suffrage amendment because he was afraid he'd lose the support of the Democratic party. In addition, his attention was taken up with the looming world war. But finally, in 1916, at Carrie Chapman Catt's emergency suffrage convention in Atlantic City, New Jersey, he told women they'd triumph eventually, but that they could wait "a little while" for the vote.

Anna Howard Shaw was having none of that. "We have waited long enough, Mr. President, for the vote," she retorted.

In 1918, President Wilson finally came out in favor of woman suffrage—the suffrage victory in New York State had made the amendment all but inevitable. Wilson presented suffrage not as a right but as a war measure, perhaps so the weight of his office would protect the amendment from legal challenges.

"It is my duty to win the war and to ask you to remove every obstacle that stands in the way of winning it," he said to members of Congress.

Still, Congress defied the president. The amendment, coming up for consideration in 1918 for the fortieth time, passed in the House but was defeated in the Senate by two votes.

In February 1919, the amendment again came up in Congress. Southern senators held out, belittling suffragists as a "petticoat brigade." They still wanted individual states to decide who could vote, so they could continue to exclude women and African Americans. Although the House again passed the amendment, it lost in the Senate—this time by one vote.

On May 19, 1919, the amendment came up for a vote during a special session of the Sixty-Sixth Congress. Again, it passed the House by a large majority. The Senate debated for several days, and on June 4, the vote was taken. This time the scales tipped—the vote was 56–25 in favor.

The suffragists had won! A huge roar of celebration from the spectators' gallery rocked the house.

But the race to gain ratification from the states was on. Approval needed a three-fourths majority. In 1919, there were forty-eight states, so thirty-six of them had to sign on. Carrie Chapman Catt didn't waste much time celebrating. "CCC danced all over the place and then settled down to THINK," a good friend noted.

Suffragists took up their pens and hit the road to lobby the states. Their hard work paid off. By March 1920, thirty-five states had given their approval.

With one more state to go, suffragists converged on Nashville, Tennessee, where the next vote would take place. If suffrage didn't win here, passage of the amendment depended on only a few possible states. The southern states had stubbornly resisted, so lobbying in the state capital was intense. Suffragists cornered members of the General Assembly in hotel lobbies, while anti-suffrage forces plied lawmakers with booze.

The State Senate passed the amendment easily by a vote of 25–4. But the House vote was uncertain. On August 17, the debate raged for hours. "Isn't it time for the South to quit being the tail-end of creation?" asked pro-suffrage Representative Tom Riddick. "We want this to remain a white man's country!" thundered anti-suffrage House Speaker Seth Walker. A vote to adjourn until the next day passed.

On August 18, two votes to table the amendment failed in a 48–48 tie. And, so, the vote for ratification began, and with each lawmaker's position firm, it looked like another tie, which would defeat the amendment. But in jumped Harry T. Burn, the "good boy" who had listened to the pleas of his mother. He had planned to vote "nay," but at his mother's urging to back suffrage, he changed his vote to "aye" for a 49–47 win.

Finally! The women had won, and the battle was over. Or so they thought.

Immediately, Walker changed his vote to aye, making it 50 for and 46 against. The change was a tactic—it granted two days for another vote to be taken. But on August 19, the call to hold another vote was defeated. And the next day, August 20, despite some creative stalling tactics by the opposition, the original vote held.

Next, anti-suffragists got an order preventing the governor from certifying the vote. They rallied for support across the state, but, in the end, a judge declared the order invalid.

On August 24, 1920, the governor signed the papers into law, and on August 26, a train carrying the Tennessee ratification certificate reached Washington, DC, where Secretary of State Bainbridge Colby quietly signed the amendment alone at his home. Everyone thought the battle was finally, truly won.

But anti-suffragists in Tennessee took their fight to higher courts, and it wasn't until 1922 that the U.S. Supreme Court finally shut them down. In the South, though, women—and African American men—continued to be harassed and turned away from the polls with the illegal use of fees, literacy tests, and land or income requirements.

Women and African Americans weren't the only people in our nation's history to be denied the vote. Native Americans had to wait another four years until the Indian Citizenship Act of 1924 allowed them to vote, and they too faced discrimination at the polls. Chinese Americans didn't become voting citizens until 1943. Three years later, people of Asian Indian ancestry gained the vote, and in 1951, Japanese Americans joined the national citizenry. In 1961, the Twenty-third Amendment granted residents of Washington, DC, the vote, and the Voting Rights Act of 1965 finally made discrimination against any eligible voter illegal. In 1971, the Twenty-sixth Amendment lowered the voting age from twenty-one to eighteen.

But even today, battles surrounding the vote continue, as politicians try to exclude voters who aren't likely to vote for them or their policies by complicating voter registration, relocating polling places, and redrawing legislative districts. Civil rights activists are continuously working to make voting a more simple, fair, and accessible act for all American citizens.

On a summer day in 1848, a group of five women met in a small Upstate New York town to air their opinions over tea. Because of that seemingly ordinary afternoon chat, 27 million women could vote legally seventy-two years later. And, today, more than 168 million American women are eligible to vote at age eighteen.

"Never doubt that a small group of thoughtful, committed citizens can change the world," said Margaret Mead, an American anthropologist who was nineteen when women won the vote. "Indeed, it is the only thing that ever has."

The cover of the program for the March 3, 1913, National American Woman Suffrage Association parade in Washington, DC, was the work of artist Benjamin Moran Dale (1889–1951).

WOMAN SUFFRAGE TIMELINE

1840 » Women delegates to the World Anti-Slavery Convention in London are barred from participating, igniting a backlash among American women (June 12–23)

1848 » Lucretia Mott, Elizabeth Cady Stanton, and three other women convene the first women's suffrage convention in Seneca Falls, NY (July 19–20)

1850 » First nationwide women's rights convention held in Worcester, MA

1866 » American Equal Rights Association (AERA) formed to secure suffrage for all U.S. citizens

1868 » Fourteenth Amendment grants citizenship to persons born or naturalized in the United States, including freed slaves, but qualifies the citizens' rights with the word "male"

1869 » AERA splits into the National Woman Suffrage Association and the American Woman Suffrage Association over the issue of giving the vote to African American men via the Fifteenth Amendment

1869 » Wyoming Territory becomes first to grant women the vote

1870 » Fifteenth Amendment gives African American men the vote

1870 » Women in Utah Territory granted franchise (revoked in 1887; reinstated in 1895)

1871 » Victoria Woodhull addresses the House Judiciary Committee, arguing women's right to vote as citizens is protected by the Fourteenth Amendment

1871 » Anti-Suffrage Party is formed to oppose woman suffrage

1872 » Susan B. Anthony arrested in Rochester, NY, for voting in presidential election

1874 » U.S. Supreme Court rules the Fourteenth Amendment does not grant women the vote

1878 » Women's suffrage amendment (Susan B. Anthony Amendment) introduced in Congress for the first time

1883 » Washington Territory grants women the vote (revoked in 1888; reinstated in 1910)

1887 » First vote on women's suffrage defeated in U.S. Senate

1890 » Suffrage groups merge into the National American Woman Suffrage Association (NAWSA)

1893 » Colorado grants women the vote

1896 » Idaho adopts woman suffrage

1902 » Women from 10 nations meet in Washington, DC, to plan international suffrage effort

1907 » Harriot Stanton Blatch organizes the Equality League of Self-Supporting Women

1908 » Two dozen members of the Progressive Woman Suffrage Union march down Broadway, New York City, despite being denied a permit (February 16)

1909 » James Lees Laidlaw forms the Men's League for Woman Suffrage

1910 » The first large-scale suffrage parade of 400 women, organized by Harriot Stanton Blatch, marches down Fifth Avenue in New York City (May 21)

1911 » 3,000 suffragists march down Fifth Avenue in New York City accompanied by floats and bands (May 6)

1912 » 10,000 suffragists march down Fifth Avenue in New York City (May 6)

1912 » 15,000 suffragists proceed down Fifth Avenue in a nighttime "Torchlight Parade" of marchers, floats, chariots, and horses lit by orange Japanese lanterns (November 9)

1912 » Oregon, Kansas, and Arizona adopt woman suffrage

1913 » A mob of angry, drunken men attacks the 8,000 marchers of the Woman's Suffrage Procession in Washington, DC, on the eve of President Wilson's inauguration, and 300 women are treated for injuries (March 3)

1913 » Alice Paul and Lucy Burns form the Congressional Committee for Woman Suffrage as a subcommittee of NAWSA (April)

1913 » Alaska Territory grants women suffrage

1914 » Nevada and Montana adopt woman suffrage

1914 » Alice Paul and Lucy Burns break away from NAWSA to found the Congressional Union for Woman Suffrage

1915 » 50,000 suffragists march down Fifth Avenue in New York City, the largest parade the city has ever seen. The parade includes 20,000 women, 2,500 men, 74 women on horseback, 143 automobiles, and 57 bands with 1,000 musicians (October 23)

1916 » The Congressional Union becomes the National Woman's Party (NWP)

1916 » Jeannette Rankin (R., Montana) becomes the first women elected to Congress in the House of Representatives (November 6)

1917 » NWP suffragists—the "Silent Sentinels"—begin demonstrations against the government. Arrests, trials, jail terms, hunger strikes, and force-feeding soon follow (January 10)

1917 » 1,000 suffragists march seven times around the White House on the day of President Wilson's second inauguration. The "Grand Picket" mirrors the march around the biblical city of Jericho that felled its walls (March 4)

1917 » 25,000 suffragists led by Carrie Chapman Catt parade down Fifth Avenue in New York City, carrying posters containing signatures of more than 1 million New York women demanding the vote (October 7)

1917 » New York State grants women the vote via constitutional amendment (November 6)

1917 » Suffragists brutalized during the Night of Terror at Occoquan Workhouse in Lorton, Virginia (November 14–15)

1918 » President Woodrow Wilson backs constitutional amendment as a war measure (September 30)

1919 » Michigan, South Dakota, and Oklahoma adopt woman suffrage

1919 » Federal woman suffrage amendment passed by the House of Representatives (May 19)

1919 » Federal woman suffrage amendment passed by the Senate (June 4)

1920 » Tennessee becomes the last of thirty-six states needed to ratify the Nineteenth Amendment (August 18)

1920 » League of Women Voters organized to guide newly enfranchised women

Even after women won the vote, several states took their time formally ratifying the Nineteenth Amendment. They were:

1941 » Maryland	**1969** » Florida	**1970** » Louisiana
1952 » Virginia	**1969** » South Carolina	**1971** » North Carolina
1953 » Alabama	**1970** » Georgia	**1984** » Mississippi

THE BANNERS THEY CARRIED

Activists have always rallied around slogans. Today, we might use hashtags like #MeToo, #NeverAgain, or #BlackLivesMatter. In the suffragists' day, banners helped to spread messages. Suffragists used their skills as seamstresses to sew sashes and banners for public events.

Mary Winsor, a suffragist from Pennsylvania, holds a banner proclaiming the suffragists' demand to be treated as political prisoners, not criminals. As political prisoners, they would have had better treatment in jail and the opportunity to take their cause to the courts. Mary Winsor served two jail terms.

A delegation of suffragists from Pennsylvania pickets in front of the White House.

Suffragists from New York State picket the White House. The women picketed in all kinds of weather—on this cold day in January, the women are wearing rain gear.

Alice Paul leads a line of picketers from the National Woman's Party headquarters to the White House. Her banner reads: "The Time Has Come To Conquer Or Submit. For Us There Is But One Choice. We Have Made It, President Wilson." Dora Lewis, a suffragist from Philadelphia who was in her seventies, follows Alice. President Wilson had just declared that picketers would receive six-month prison sentences.

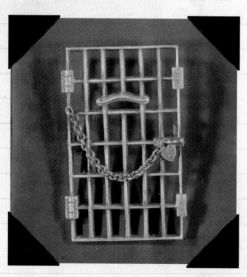

Alice Paul asked artist Nina Allender to design a pin honoring suffragists who were jailed for picketing the White House. Each of the 168 suffragists who were jailed received one of these silver pins.

Virginia Arnold, a suffragist from North Carolina, holds a banner likening President Woodrow Wilson to a tyrant. This banner incited a near riot when it was unfurled in front of the White House.

PLACES TO VISIT

WOMEN'S RIGHTS NATIONAL HISTORICAL PARK » Seneca Falls, New York
Landmarks of the 1848 Seneca Falls convention are open, including the Wesleyan Methodist Chapel, Elizabeth Cady Stanton's house, and the home of Mary Ann M'Clintock, another organizer of the Seneca Falls convention.

THE NATIONAL MUSEUM OF AMERICAN HISTORY » Washington, DC
The "American Democracy: A Great Leap of Faith" exhibit contains artifacts from the battle for the women's vote, including banners, posters, pins, and a suffrage wagon.

THE PORTRAIT MONUMENT » Washington, DC
A statue portraying Stanton, Anthony, and Mott stands in the Capitol Rotunda. It was commissioned by the National Woman's Party in 1920 and carved by Adelaide Johnson, but was in storage until 1997.

SOJOURNER TRUTH MEMORIAL » Florence, Massachusetts
The abolitionist and women's rights champion is memorialized with a statue here.

FREDERICK DOUGLASS HOUSE » Washington, DC
Cedar Hill was the last home of the former slave and antislavery activist. The home and exhibits and an interpretive film are available for visitors.

SUSAN B. ANTHONY HOUSE » Rochester, New York
Home of the women's suffrage and civil rights leader and site of her arrest for voting in a presidential election.

THE MATILDA JOSLYN GAGE HOME AND FOUNDATION » Fayetteville, New York
Gage's home as an adult is now a museum, research facility, and educational foundation that contains Native American, Underground Railroad, and other exhibits.

THE FRANCES WILLARD HOUSE MUSEUM AND WILLARD MEMORIAL LIBRARY AND ARCHIVES » Evanston, Illinois
Rest Cottage was Willard's family home from the age of eighteen and the headquarters of the Woman's Christian Temperance Union. A statue of Willard also stands in National Statuary Hall in the U.S. Capitol Building in Washington, DC.

CARRIE CHAPMAN CATT GIRLHOOD HOME AND MUSEUM » Charles City, Iowa
Visitors can tour Catt's childhood home, gain information in the interpretive center, and walk through the surrounding apple orchards and native prairie.

MARY CHURCH TERRELL MEMORIAL » Washington, DC
Plaques at Terrell Place (7th and F Streets) commemorate Terrell's civil rights activism, including the sit-ins she led at Hecht's Department Store, which was once at this site. A book about her life is available for visitors in the lobby of the building.

BELMONT-PAUL WOMEN'S EQUALITY NATIONAL MONUMENT » Washington, DC
Headquarters of the National Woman's Party from 1929 onward. It contains National Woman's Party information and suffrage artifacts and an extensive collection of Nina Allender's artwork for *The Suffragist*. Two stone steps from the Occoquan Workhouse are displayed here.

CAMERON HOUSE » Washington, DC
This house at 21 Madison Place NW was the headquarters of Alice Paul's National Woman's Party while the Silent Sentinels picketed the White House. Today it is the Benjamin Ogle Tayloe House. The house is not open to the public, but from its front door, the White House gates can be seen, as well as the statue of Lafayette under which suffragists staged protests.

LUCY BURNS MUSEUM » Lorton, Virginia
This museum in a renovated building of the Occoquan Workhouse (also called the Lorton Reformatory) displays original jail cells and a history of the suffragists' imprisonment. It is on the campus of the Workhouse Arts Center, part of the Northern Virginia Arts and Culture District.

JEANNETTE RANKIN STATUE » Washington, DC
Jeannette Rankin's statue is one of two statues contributed by the state of Montana to the National Statuary Hall in the U.S. Capitol Building.

PAULSDALE AND THE ALICE PAUL INSTITUTE » Mount Laurel, New Jersey
Alice Paul's childhood home is open for tours and contains an exhibit and a video of her suffrage work. The Institute's library is available to researchers.

NOTES

Introduction

11 "In the first presidential election": Jill Lepore, "Rock, Paper, Scissors: How We Used to Vote," *New Yorker,* October 13, 2008, https://www.newyorker.com/magazine/2008/10/13/rock-paper-scissors.

12 "In the presidential election that year": Elaine Weiss, *The Woman's Hour: The Great Fight to Win the Vote* (New York: Viking, 2018), p. 325.

1. Lucretia Coffin Mott

14 "Quakerism does not mean quietism": Lucretia Mott, speech, annual meeting of the Pennsylvania Anti-Slavery Society, October 25–26, 1860. Reported in the *National Anti-Slavery Standard*, November 3, 1860. *The Standard* was the weekly newspaper of the American Anti-Slavery Society.

15 "I resolved to claim": Constance Buell Burnett, *Five for Freedom: The Crusade for Woman's Rights* (New York, Abelard Press, 1953), p. 23.

15 "If our principles are right": Burnett, *Five for Freedom*, p. 31.

16 "The discussion grew more bitter": Elizabeth Cady Stanton, Susan B. Anthony, and Matilda Joslyn Gage, *History of Woman Suffrage* (New York: Fowler and Wells, 1881), vol. 1, p. 54. As the book was coauthored by the three women, it's impossible to say which one of them made this comment, although Elizabeth was known as the writer of the group.

16 "a Convention to discuss": "Women's Rights Convention," ad placed in the *Seneca County Courier*, July 14, 1848. Frederick Douglass ran the same ad in his Rochester, NY, newspaper, *The North Star*.

16 "We hold these truths": Declaration of Sentiments and Resolutions, the document that arose from the Seneca Falls Women's Rights Convention on July 19–20, 1848. As reported in *The North Star* on July 28, 1848.

17 "I am no advocate": Mott, *National Anti-Slavery Standard*.

2. Sojourner Truth

18 "I was to declare": Harriet Beecher Stowe, "Sojourner Truth, The Libyan Sibyl," *Atlantic Monthly* (April 1863), p. 478.

19 "Oh! my God!": Sojourner Truth, *Narrative of Sojourner Truth* (Boston: J. B. Yerrinton and Son, 1850), p. 26.

19 "Ah! The slaveholders": Truth, *Narrative of Sojourner Truth*, p. 39.

20 "I was to declare": Beecher Stowe, "The Libyan Sibyl," p. 478.

21 "Man is in a tight place": Sojourner Truth, "Ain't I a Woman?" speech, women's rights convention in Akron, Ohio, as reported on June 21, 1851, by Marcus Robinson, editor of the Anti-Slavery Bugle. Later reports of the speech change her words dramatically, giving her southern speech patterns that wouldn't have been hers as a northern-born woman.

21 "Well, if woman upset the world": Truth, *"Ain't I a Woman?"*

21 "You may hiss": Sojourner Truth, speech, Woman's Rights Convention, Broadway Tabernacle, New York City, September 6–7, 1853. This convention is known as the "Mob Convention," due to the hatred and violence directed at the women in attendance.

3. Abby Kelley Foster

22 "Harmony? I don't want harmony": "Convention on Taxation Without Representation" held in Worcester, MA, before the February 20, 1874, auction. Dorothy Sterling, *Ahead of Her Time: Abby Kelley and the Politics of Antislavery* (New York: W. W. Norton, 1991), p. 369.

23 "This Jezebel": Lucy Stone, *"The Progress of Fifty Years"*, speech, Women's Pavilion, World's Columbian Exposition, Chicago, May 1–October 30, 1898. She likely gave this speech many times, not just on one date. The Exposition was a six-month celebration of Columbus's arrival in the New World and was like a World's Fair. In the Old Testament, Jezebel is presented as an evil woman, a foreign queen of Israel who has Jewish prophets and worshippers murdered.

24 "God will smite you": Sterling, *Ahead of Her Time*, p. 65. Abolitionist Theodore Dwight Weld said this to Abby after her speech at the Anti-Slavery Convention of American Women held in Philadelphia on May 17, 1838. It is believed to be her first public speech.

24 "It is the still small voice": Abby Kelley Foster, speech, May 17, 1838, Philadelphia. Margaret Hope Bacon, *I Speak for My Slave Sister: The Life of Abby Kelley Foster* (New York: Thomas Y. Crowell, 1974), p. 33.

25 "Harmony? I don't want harmony": Sterling, *Ahead of Her Time*, p. 362.

25 "Now feeble by advancing age": Sterling, *Ahead of Her Time*, p. 369.

25 "Bloody feet, Sisters": Address to the National Woman's Rights Convention in Worcester, MA, October 16, 1851. Sterling, *Ahead of Her Time*, p. 268.

4. Elizabeth Cady Stanton

26 "The thinking minds": Elizabeth Cady Stanton, Address to the New York State Legislature, adopted by the Woman's Rights Convention, Albany, New York, February 14–15, 1854.

27 "When you are grown up": Elizabeth Cady Stanton, *Eighty Years and More* (New York: European Publishing, 1898), p. 32. Many versions of this story exist, and Elizabeth may have embellished it in her memoir. It is unlikely that her father, who was upset by Elizabeth's activism as an adult, would have encouraged her as a child to speak in public.

27 "Oh my daughter": Stanton, *Eighty Years*, p. 20.

28 "were in agony": Stanton, *Eighty Years*, p. 80.

28 "I pace up and down": Ellen Carol DuBois, ed., *The Elizabeth Cady Stanton-Susan B. Anthony Reader, Correspondence, Writings, Speeches* (Boston: Northeastern University Press, 1992), p. 63. For a more complete compilation of the women's writings, see the six-volume set, *The Selected Papers of Elizabeth Cady Stanton and Susan B. Anthony*, edited by Ann D. Gordon (New Brunswick, NJ: Rutgers University Press, 1997–2013).

28 "The right is ours": Stanton's address on woman's rights in September 1848 in Waterloo, NY, just months after the Seneca Falls convention. It is perhaps the first speech she ever gave on women's rights.

28 "As in the war": Elizabeth Cady Stanton, "Address to the First Anniversary of the American Equal Rights Association," speech, May 9, 1867.

29 "How I wish I could see you": Letter to Susan B. Anthony, November 30, 1872, as quoted in Lori D. Ginzberg, *Elizabeth Cady Stanton: An American Life* (New York: Hill and Wang, 2009), p. 152.

5. Lucy Stone

30 "Justice, simple justice": Agnes E. Ryan. *"The Torch Bearer: A Look Forward and Back at the Woman's Journal, the Organ of the Woman's Movement."* (Boston: *The Woman's Journal and Suffrage News*, 1916), p. 10.

31 "Is the child crazy?": Alice Stone Blackwell, *Lucy Stone: Pioneer of Woman's Rights*. (Charlottesville: University of Virginia Press, 2001), p. 16. Alice was Lucy's daughter.

32 "that little blue-eyed girl": James McKinney letter, *Woman's Journal*, June 14, 1902, as reported in Andrea Moore Kerr, *Lucy Stone: Speaking Out for Equality* (New Brunswick, NJ: Rutgers University Press, 1992), p. 38.

32 "It only shows me": Reminiscences of Anna Watkins, a classmate of young Lucy's. Blackwell Family Papers, Container 87, Library of Congress Manuscript Division, Washington, DC.

32 "I go for all sharing": Abraham Lincoln, letter to the editor, *Sagamom* (Illinois) Journal, June 13, 1836, as quoted in Phillip Stern, ed., *The Life and Writings of Abraham Lincoln* (New York: Modern Library, 1942), p. 225.

33 "Leave women, then": Lucy Stone, "Disappointment Is the Lot of Women," speech, women's rights convention, Cincinnati, Ohio, October 17, 1855.

6. Julia Ward Howe

34 "Now, I say": Julia Ward Howe, "The Moral Initiative as Related to Woman," address before the World's Congress of Representative Women, World's Columbian Exposition, Chicago, Illinois, May 16, 1893.

35 "My daughter": Laura Elizabeth Howe Richards, Maud Howe, and Florence Howe Hall, *Julia Ward Howe, 1819–1910* (Boston: Houghton Mifflin, 1915), vol. 1, p. 36. The authors were Julia's daughters.

35 "This is my little girl": Julia Ward Howe, *Reminiscences, 1819–1899* (Boston: Houghton Mifflin, 1899), p. 14.

36 "Among the shining I have shone": Julia Ward Howe, "The Heart's Astronomy," in *Passion-Flowers* (Boston: Ticknor, Reed and Fields, 1854), p. 102.

36 "Oh! had I known earlier": Julia Ward Howe, *Reminiscences*, p. 373.

37 "The weapon of Christian warfare": Julia Ward Howe, "Woman and the Suffrage: The Case for Woman Suffrage," *The American Journal of Nursing*, vol. 9, no. 8 (May 1909), p. 566. Reprinted from *The Outlook*, April 3, 1909, a weekly newspaper that focused on social and political issues.

37 "Make your protest": Julia Ward Howe, "Woman and the Suffrage," p. 566.

37 "she forms a bridge": Laura Elizabeth Howe Richards, Maud Howe, and Florence Howe Hall, *Julia Ward Howe, 1819–1910*, p. 360.

7. Susan B. Anthony

38 "No man is good enough": Ida Husted Harper, *The Life and Work of Susan B. Anthony* (Indianapolis, IN: The Hollenbeck Press, 1898), vol. 2, p. 83.

39 "Baked 21 loaves of bread": Penny Colman, *Elizabeth Cady Stanton and Susan B. Anthony: A Friendship that Changed the World* (New York: Square Fish, 2016), p. 27. From Susan's diary.

40 "I vowed then and there": "Champion of Her Sex," an interview with reporter Nellie Bly, *The* (New York) *World*, February 2, 1896, p. 10.

40 "Men, their rights": Motto on the masthead of *The Revolution*, starting with the second edition. The magazine was published from January 1868 to February 1872.

40 "literary nitroglycerin": Burnett, *Five for Freedom*, p. 170.

40 "Now wouldn't it be splendid": Letter to Isabella Beecher Hooker, April 9, 1874. University of Rochester Department of Rare Books, Special Collections and Preservation, Rochester, NY.

41 "aristocracy of sex": Elizabeth Cady Stanton, "Declaration of Rights of the Women of the United States," speech, given on behalf of the National Woman Suffrage Association at the nation's Jubilee celebration, Philadelphia, July 4, 1876.

41 "Let women be first": Susan made this remark in a debate with Frederick Douglass at a meeting of the American Equal Rights Association May 12–13, 1869. David W. Blight, *Frederick Douglass: Prophet of Freedom* (New York: Simon & Schuster, 2018), p. 491. She adopted the phrase from George Francis Train, the openly racist financial backer of *The Revolution*.

41 "When women, because they are women": Frederick Douglass, "Let No One Be Excluded from the Ballot Box," *The Frederick Douglass Papers*, ed. John W. Blassingame (New Haven, CT: Yale University Press, 1991), series 1, vol. 4, p. 216–17.

41 "Put into the hands of all women": Susan B. Anthony, "Woman Wants Bread, Not the Ballot," speech given on many occasions.

41 "Well, I have been": Letter to Elizabeth Cady Stanton, November 5, 1872. *"Remarkable Works, Remarkable Times: Highlights from the Huntington Library,"* Huntington Library, Art Collections and Botanical Gardens, San Marino, CA.

41 "Failure is impossible!": Susan's last public address at a celebration of her eighty-sixth birthday in Washington, DC, February 1906. Harriet Eaton, ed., *The Handbook and Proceedings of the National American Woman Suffrage Association* (Washington, DC: NAWSA Publishing, 1906).

8. Isabella Beecher Hooker

42 "It is the plain duty": Isabella Beecher Hooker, "The Constitutional Rights of the Women of the United States," speech, the International Council of Women, Washington, DC, March 30, 1883.

43 "The writer pointed out": A paraphrase of Thomas Wentworth Higginson, "Ought Women to Learn the Alphabet?" *Atlantic Monthly*, vol. 3, no. 16 (February 1859), p. 14. Higginson was an abolitionist and women's rights advocate.

44 "a hopeless mystery": Isabella Beecher Hooker, "The Last of the Beechers: Memories on My Eighty-Third Birthday," *Connecticut Magazine*, vol. 9 (Spring 1905), p. 291.

44 "I would not open the polls": Isabella Beecher Hooker, "Shall Women Vote? A Matrimonial Dialogue." The article was written in February 1860, but never published. Isabella showed the essay to Higginson, but he wasn't able to help her. She had included ideas that he thought too radical to appeal to magazine editors.

44 "With equal political rights": Hooker, "The Last of the Beechers," p. 295.

44 "My sister's book": Hooker, "The Last of the Beechers," p. 295.

44 "Can anything be plainer": Beecher Hooker, "The Constitutional Rights."

9. Mary Ann Shadd Cary

46 "Millions of colored women today": Mary Ann Shadd Cary, speech before the House Judiciary Committee, Mary Ann Shadd Cary Papers, Moorland-Spingarn Research Center, Howard University, Series F, Box 13-1. She also reported on the event in *The New National Era*, February 5, 1874.

47 "Coming down Broadway": Frederick Douglass, "Ethiop," in *Frederick Douglass' Paper*, November 9, 1855, as noted in Jim Bearden and Linda Jean Butler, *Shadd: The Life and Times of Mary Shadd Cary* (Toronto: NC Press, 1977), p. 20. The newspaper was created in 1851 by the merger of Douglass's *The North Star*, which had been founded in 1847, with the Syracuse, NY, Liberty Party Paper.

48 "We should do more": Mary Ann Shadd, letter, *The North Star*, March 23, 1849.

48 "Millions of colored women today": Shadd Cary, *The New National Era*.

49 "'Better whiskey and more of it'": Interview, *The Voice*, October 23, 1890. *The Voice* was a temperance newspaper published in New York.

49 "Think of Patrick and Sambo": Elizabeth Cady Stanton, opening address, third annual meeting of the American Equal Rights Association, May 12, 1869, New York City.

49 "For all these ignorant, alien peoples": Susan B. Anthony, speech before the Senate Select Committee on Women Suffrage, February 18, 1902. The hearing accompanied the annual introduction of a resolution proposing an amendment to the Constitution giving women the vote. Washington, DC: Government Printing Office, 1902.

49 "some American people left": "Conversations with Alice Paul: Woman Suffrage and the Equal Rights Amendment," an interview by Amelia Frye (1972–73), Suffragists Oral History Project, Bancroft Library, University of California at Berkeley, p. 11.

49 "Mary A. S. Cary": Stanton, Anthony, and Gage, *History of Woman Suffrage*, vol. 3, p. 73.

49 "Who shall overrule": Mary Ann Shadd Cary, "Break Every Yoke and Let the Oppressed

Go Free," sermon given on April 6, 1858. Philip S. Foner and Robert J. Branham, eds., *Lift Every Voice: African American Oratory, 1787–1900* (Tuscaloosa: University of Alabama Press, 1997), p. 318.

10. Matilda Joslyn Gage

50 "I think I was born": Matilda Joslyn Gage, speech, first meeting of the International Council of Women, March 25, 1888, Washington, DC. The National Woman Suffrage Association started the council after Elizabeth Cady Stanton and Susan B. Anthony visited Europe in 1882. The council is still in operation today, seeking human rights for women worldwide.

51 "I think I was born": Gage, International Council of Women.

52 "satanic": Sally Roesch Wagner, ed., introduction to *Woman, Church and State: A Historical Account of the Status of Woman through the Christian Ages: With Reminiscences of the Matriarchate*, by Matilda Joslyn Gage (Watertown, MA: Persephone Press, 1980), p. xv.

52 "Never was justice": Matilda Joslyn Gage, "The Remnant of the Five Nations: Woman's Rights Among the Indians," *New York Evening Post*, September 24, 1875. The article was part of a series written by Matilda.

52 "The soul must assert": Matilda Joslyn Gage, *Woman, Church and State* (New York: The Truth Seeker Company, 1893), p. 243.

53 "Heavenly Father and Mother": Margaret Stanton Lawrence, "Reminiscences," Stanton Collection, Vassar College Library, Poughkeepsie, NY. Margaret was one of Elizabeth Cady Stanton's daughters.

11. Frances Willard

54 "It is good for boys and girls": Frances Willard, *Glimpses of Fifty Years: The Autobiography of an American Woman* (Chicago: H. J. Smith & Co., 1889), p. 43.

55 "It is good for boys and girls" Willard, *Glimpses of Fifty Years*, p. 43.

56 "Girls should be definitely": Willard, *Glimpses of Fifty Years*, p. 124.

56 "the guns are ballots": Willard, *Glimpses of Fifty Years*, p. 445.

56 "We do not propose to trail our skirts": WCTU leader Lucy Butler, quoted in Ruth Bordin, *Frances Willard: A Biography* (Chapel Hill: University of North Carolina Press, 1986), p. 103.

56 "clad in the garments of power": Frances Willard, *Women and Temperance: Or, The Work and Workers of the Woman's Christian Temperance Union* (Hartford, CT: Park Publishing Co., 1883), p. 459. This book contains a version of what was known as Frances's "Home Protection Speech," which she gave on numerous occasions.

57 "in order to gain favor": Alfreda M. Duster, ed., *Crusade for Justice: The Autobiography of Ida B. Wells* (Chicago: University of Chicago Press, 1970), p. 151.

57 "I find great good": Willard, *Glimpses of Fifty Years*, p. 627.

57 "I can speak and work": Letter written by Susan B. Anthony and Elizabeth Cady Stanton to Isabella Beecher Hooker, October 11, 1869. University of Rochester Department of Rare Books, Special Collections, and Preservation, Rochester, NY.

12. Anna Howard Shaw

58 "Women must have power": Anna Howard Shaw, "Equal Suffrage: A Problem of Political Justice." *The Annals of the American Academy of Political and Social Science*, vol. 56 (Women in Public Life), November 1914, p. 97.

59 "I'll be damned if I take you": Anna Howard Shaw, D.D., M.D., *The Story of a Pioneer* (New York: Harper & Bros, 1915), p. 78.

59 "He gave no thought": Shaw, *Pioneer*, p. 27.

60 "It was a wonderful moment": Shaw, *Pioneer*, p. 55.

60 "a lighted match applied to gunpowder": Shaw, *Pioneer*, p. 62.

60 "In the people's voice": Anna Howard Shaw, "Fundamental Principles of a Republic," speech, Albany, NY, June 21, 1915. Anna gave the speech while New York State was considering woman suffrage.

61 "the hardships we underwent": Shaw, *Pioneer*, p. 191.

61 "I have not yet won": Shaw, *Pioneer*, p. 121.

61 "There are many men": From the mission statement of the league's founding document, reprinted in the *St. John's Globe*, New Brunswick, Canada, on May 17, 1912. The quote was included in a column by playwright George Middleton, the husband of actress and suffragist Fola La Follette. There is no known copy of the document itself.

61 "Tagging after the girls": "Him," "How It Feels to Be the Husband of a Suffragist" (New York: George H. Doran Co., 1915). NAWSA Collection, Digital Image 5, Rare Book and Special Collections Division, Library of Congress Online Catalog. This humorous booklet was written anonymously by the husband of a suffragist and supporter of woman suffrage.

13. Carrie Chapman Catt

62 "Women arise: Demand the Vote!": Carrie Chapman Catt, "The Crisis," speech, emergency convention of NAWSA, Atlantic City, NJ, September 7, 1916. This version of her quote is from *The Woman's Journal and Suffrage News*, September 16, 1916.

63 "Why, Mother": Mary Gray Peck, *Carrie Chapman Catt: A Biography* (New York: H. W. Wilson, 1944), p. 28.

64 "I have a voice like a foghorn": *Not for Ourselves Alone: The Story of Elizabeth Cady Stanton & Susan B. Anthony*, a documentary by Ken Burns produced in conjunction with National Public Radio and the Public Broadcasting Service in 1999.

64 "escapers from the insane asylums": Carrie Chapman Catt, "Only Yesterday," unfinished manuscript. Catt Papers, Sophia Smith Collection, Smith College, Northampton, MA.

65 "We women demand an equal voice": Carrie Chapman Catt, speech, suffrage conference, Stockholm, Sweden, June 11, 1911.

65 "My husband needs me now": Peck, *Carrie Chapman Catt*, p. 143. Carrie nursed her husband in his dying days but also began organizing the International World Suffrage Alliance, which continues today as the International Alliance of Women. Susan B. Anthony worked alongside Carrie in the IWSA.

65 "Women arise: Demand the vote!": Catt, "The Crisis."

65 "This is not a movement": Henry Allen, a former governor of Kansas, who gave speeches before and after the parade. As quoted in Peck, *Carrie Chapman Catt*, p. 231.

65 "By 1919, fifteen states": Jacqueline Van Voris, *Carrie Chapman Catt: A Public Life* (New York: The Feminist Press at The City University of New York, 1987), p. 153.

65 "You've won!": Carrie Chapman Catt, speech, Chicago "Victory Convention," February 15, 1920. As quoted in Barbara Stuhler, *For the Public Record: A Documentary History of the League of Women Voters* (Westport, CT: Greenwood Press, 2000), p. 32.

65 "We are no longer petitioners": Carrie Chapman Catt, speech, "Votes for Women" celebration, New York City, August 27, 1920, following ratification of the Nineteenth Amendment. As quoted in Peck, *Carrie Chapman Catt*, p. 342. Arriving at New York's Penn Station, Carrie was greeted by Governor Al Smith, who escorted her in a victory parade to the Waldorf Astoria Hotel.

14. Ida B. Wells-Barnett

66 "With no sacredness of the ballot": Ida B. Wells-Barnett, "How Enfranchisement Stops Lynchings," *Original Rights*, vol. 1, no. 4, June 1910, p. 45.

67 "After being a light-hearted school girl": Alfreda M. Duster, ed., Crusade for Justice: *The Autobiography of Ida B. Wells* (Chicago: Chicago University Press, 1970), pp. 15–16.

68 "The moment he caught hold of my arm": Duster, *Crusade for Justice*, p. 18.

68 "It was through journalism": Paula Giddings, *Ida: A Sword Among Lions: Ida B. Wells and the Campaign Against Lynching* (New York: HarperCollins, 2009), p. 69.

68 "The way to right wrongs": The slogan is from an 1892 ad in the *Washington Bee* newspaper for a lecture titled "Southern Mob Rule" that Ida gave at Metropolitan AME Church in Washington, DC, on October 31, 1892. Mary Church Terrell presided at the event.

68 "To a woman brought up as I was": Sylvia D. Hoffert, *Alva Vanderbilt Belmont: Unlikely Champion of Women's Rights* (Bloomington: Indiana University Press, 2011), p. 85.

69 "suffrage sentiment doubled overnight": Adade Mitchell Wheeler, "Conflict in Illinois: The Woman Suffrage Movement of 1913," *Journal of the Illinois State Historical Society*, vol. 76 (Summer 1983), p. 95.

15. Mary Church Terrell

70 "When the world takes a step forward": Mary Church Terrell, "Circular Issued: Stir Created in the Woman's Suffrage Association," *Evening Star* (Washington, DC), February 10, 1900, p. 6. Mary repeated this phrase later in *The Crisis*, the newspaper of the National Association for the Advancement of Colored People, an organization that still exists today.

71 "Haven't I got a pretty face too?": Mary Church Terrell, *A Colored Woman in a White World* (New York: G.K. Hall, 1996), p. 22. Mary originally self-published her book in 1940.

72 "The word 'people' has been turned and twisted": Terrell, "Circular Issued," p. 12.

72 "It gives me satisfaction": Terrell, *A Colored Woman*, p. 144.

73 "Graceful, elegant, logical": An endorsement of Mary on a poster advertising a lecture she gave on June 22, 1905, at Bethel A.M.E. Church, location unspecified. From Mary Church Terrell Papers, Miscellany, 1851–1954, Library of Congress, Manuscript Division, Mss. 42549, Box 41, Reel 29, Image 4.

73 "And so, lifting as we climb": Mary Church Terrell, "The Progress of Colored Women," speech given on behalf of NAWSA, February 18, 1898, the fiftieth anniversary of the Seneca Falls convention. She also gave the opening speech of the convention celebrating the sixtieth anniversary on May 27, 1908.

73 "Whatever is unusual is called unnatural": Terrell, "Circular Issued," p. 12.

73 "It was gradually borne in upon us": Harriot Stanton Blatch, "The Equality League of Self-Supporting Women Report for Year 1908–09." Library of Congress, Miller NAWSA Suffrage Scrapbooks, 1897 to 1911, Scrapbook 7 (1908 to 1909), p. 5.

16. Lucy Burns

74 "We went to jail": "A Jubilee Dinner for the Pickets," *The Suffragist*, December 15, 1917, p. 11.

75 "I was very much impressed": "Lucy Burns Tells Why English Women Have Become Militant Suffragists," *Brooklyn Daily Eagle*, June 21, 1913, p. 20.

75 "We sleepy Americans don't know": *Vassar Bulletin*, sixth annual edition, 1908, p. 8.

77 "I was held down by five people": Doris Stevens, *Jailed for Freedom* (Troutdale, OR: NewSage Press, 1995), p. 125. At the back of this book, there's a fascinating list of the 168 suffragists who spent time in jail, noting where they lived and their occupation, if they had one.

77 "She was a thousand times more valiant than I": "Conversations with Alice Paul: Woman Suffrage and the Equal Rights Amendment," interview by Amelia Frye (1972–73), Suffragists Oral History Project, Bancroft Library, University of California at Berkeley, p. 48.

77 "We have sacrificed everything we possessed": Christine A. Lunardini, *From Equal Suffrage to Equal Rights: Alice Paul and the National Woman's Party, 1910–1928* (New York: New York University Press, 1986), p. 152.

77 "They think there is nothing in our souls": Inez Haynes Irwin, *Up Hill with Banners Flying* (Penobscot, ME: Traversity Press, 1964), p. 284.

17. Jeannette Rankin

78 "I may be the first woman member of Congress": "Illinois Night is Celebrated By Nation's Suffragists," *Chicago Examiner*, December 2, 1913, p. 6.

79 "If you can take care of Jeannette": Norma Smith, *Jeannette Rankin: America's Conscience* (Helena: Montana Historical Society Press, 2002), p. 34.

79 "I was a very poor student": "Activist for World Peace, Women's Rights, and Democratic Government," interview with Jeannette Rankin conducted in 1972 by Malca Chall and Hannah Josephson, Suffragists Oral History Project, Bancroft Library, University of California at Berkeley, p. 282.

80 "Go! Go! Go!": Smith, *Jeannette Rankin*, p. 46. From Jeannette's diary.

80 "My God, that woman again!": Smith, *Jeannette Rankin*, p. 53.

80 "Once in a while": Letter written by suffragist Mary O'Neill, quoted in Smith, *Jeannette Rankin*, p. 94.

81 "How shall we answer their challenge": *Congressional Record*, Second Session of the 65th Congress, House of Representatives, January 10, 1918, p. 772.

18. Adelina Otero-Warren

82 "I will take a stand": Letter to Alice Paul, December 4, 1917, National Woman's Party Papers (NWPP), Reel 53, Woman's Collection of the Blagg-Huey Library, Texas Women's University.

84 "high spirited and independent": Ann M. Massmann, "Adelina 'Nina' Otero-Warren: A Spanish-American Cultural Broker," *Journal of the Southwest* vol. 42, no. 4 (2000), p. 882.

84 "I am with you now and always!": Letter to Alice Paul, NWPP.

84 "trade their good looks": John J. Kenney Professional Papers, A. M. Bergere Papers, New Mexico State Records Center and Archives, Santa Fe.

85 "Situation in Senate favorable": Telegram to Alice Paul, February 17, 1920, NWPP, Texas Women's University.

19. Alice Paul

86 "It is worth sacrificing everything for": Alice Paul letter to suffragist Alice Henkle, May 24, 1918, NWPP.

87 "I never met anybody": "Conversations with Alice Paul: Woman Suffrage and the Equal Rights Amendment," interview by Amelia Frye (1972-73), Suffragists Oral History Project, Bancroft Library, University of California at Berkeley, p. 15.

88 "If particular care and attention": Abigail Adams letter to John Adams. Adams was in Philadelphia for the Second Continental Congress, during which the Declaration of Independence and the Articles of Confederation, which established a national government for the United States, were crafted. The Constitution replaced the Articles of Confederation in 1789 and has been amended twenty-seven times. The first ten amendments are known as the Bill of Rights.

88 "Truth must be common to all": *Mary Wollstonecraft, A Vindication of the Rights of Woman: With Strictures on Political and Moral Subjects* (Boston: Peter Edes, 1792), p. 5.

88 "She possessed more influence": *History of Woman Suffrage*, vol. 1, appendix to chapter 1, "Preceding Causes," p. 801.

88 "Votes for women!": E. Sylvia Pankhurst, *The Suffragette* (New York: Sturgis & Walton Co., 1911), p. 459.

89 "Dear Alice, I wish to make a protest": Letter to Alice Paul from her mother, Tacie Paul, January 13, 1917, NWPP, Library of Congress, Washington, DC.

89 "Don't let them tell you": Note written by suffragist Rose Winslow and smuggled out of the Washington, DC, District Jail, NWPP. The note is not dated but is believed to have been written in November 1917. An American writer of the time, Djuna Barnes,

submitted to force feeding and wrote about the experience. "It is utterly impossible to describe the anguish of it," she wrote in her September 6, 1914, article for *The World* magazine (p. 5).

89 "It is worth sacrificing everything for": Letter to Alice Henkle, NWPP.

89 "Your place in history is assured": Walter Clark, Chief Justice of the Supreme Court of North Carolina, telegram, June 4, 1919, NWPP.

89 "Suffrage was granted to women": Tacie Paul's scrapbook, Alice Paul Papers, Arthur and Elizabeth Schlesinger Library on the History of Women in America, Box 14, Folder 211.

20. And Don't Forget

91 "It is mockery to talk of liberty": Parker Pillsbury, speech, first anniversary of the American Equal Rights Association (AERA), New York City, May 9–10, 1867, "Proceedings of the American Equal Rights Association" (New York: Robert J. Johnston, 1867), p. 38. National American Woman Suffrage Association Collection, Rare Book and Special Collections Division, Library of Congress, Washington, DC. AERA was formed in 1866 at the eleventh annual National Women's Rights Convention to secure equal rights for all citizens.

92 "She is absolutely in the hands": "Woman Suffrage Movement," editorial, *The New National Era*, October 20, 1870. Frederick Douglass published the newspaper in the early 1870s.

93 "Aim to make the World Better": "Mrs. Ruffin, Who Was Abused by Club Women at Milwaukee," *San Francisco Chronicle*, July 1, 1900, p. 26.

94 "Come, let us reason together": "Vassar Meets in Graveyard," *The Woman's Journal*, June 13, 1908.

95 "I knew that a mother's advice": Harry Burn, speech delivered to the House the day after the vote, as recounted in "Proud of Opportunity to Free American Women from Political Slavery," *The Chattanooga* (Tennessee) *News*, August 19, 1920, p. 1.

95 "Every fiber of my being rebelled": Charlotte Woodward Pierce, 1920 interview with journalist Rheta Childe Dorr, the first editor of the National Woman's Party newspaper, *The Suffragist*.

Epilogue

97 "We have waited long enough": Mary Gray Peck, *Carrie Lane Chapman Catt: A Biography* (New York: H. W. Wilson, 1944), p. 261.

97 "It is my duty to win the war": President Woodrow Wilson, address to the Senate, September 30, 1918.

98 "CCC danced all over the place": Clara Hyde letter to Mary Gray Peck, June 5, 1919, NAWSA Papers, Library of Congress.

98 "Isn't it time for the South. . . . We want this to remain a white man's country!": Elaine Weiss, *The Woman's Hour: The Great Fight to Win the Vote* (New York: Viking, 2018), pp. 284, 289.

99 "And, today, more than 168 million": The estimate of the population of women in the United States comes from the Population Division of the United Nations Department of Economic and Social Affairs, Live Country Meters, 2019.

99 "Never doubt that a small group": The origin of this famous quote from Margaret Mead cannot be pinned to any one source. It is believed she said it on many occasions.

SOURCES

Anderson, Dale. *The Seneca Falls Women's Rights Convention.* Milwaukee, WI: World Almanac Library, 2004.

Bacon, Margaret Hope. *Valiant Friend: The Life of Lucretia Mott.* New York: Walker, 1980.

Bacon, Margaret Hope. *I Speak for My Slave Sister: The Life of Abby Kelley Foster.* New York: Thomas Y. Crowell, 1974.

Baker, Jean H. *Sisters: The Lives of America's Suffragists.* New York: Hill and Wang, 2005.

Barker-Benfield, G. J., and Catherine Clinton. *Portraits of American Women: From Settlement to the Present.* New York: St. Martin's Press, 1991.

Bausum, Ann. *With Courage and Cloth: Winning the Fight for a Woman's Right to Vote.* Washington, DC: National Geographic Children's Books, 2004.

Bearden, Jim, and Linda Jean Butler. *Shadd: The Life and Times of Mary Shadd Cary.* Toronto: New Canada Publications, 1977.

Blackwell, Alice Stone. *Lucy Stone: Pioneer of Women's Rights.* Charlottesville: University Press of Virginia, 2001.

Blight, David W. *Frederick Douglass: Prophet of Freedom.* New York: Simon & Schuster, 2018.

Bordin, Ruth. *Frances Willard: A Biography.* Chapel Hill: University of North Carolina Press, 1986.

Brammer, Leila R. *Excluded from Suffrage History: Matilda Joslyn Gage, Nineteenth-Century American Feminist.* Westport, CT: Greenwood Press, 2000.

Burnett, Constance Buel. *Five for Freedom: The Crusade for Woman's Rights.* New York: Abelard Press, 1953.

Campbell, Susan. *Tempest-Tossed: The Spirit of Isabella Beecher Hooker.* Middletown, CT: Wesleyan University Press, 2014.

Carson, Mary Kay. *Why Couldn't Susan B. Anthony Vote?* New York: Sterling Children's Books, 2015.

Colman, Penny. *Elizabeth Cady Stanton and Susan B. Anthony: A Friendship That Changed the World.* New York: Square Fish, 2016.

Conkling, Winifred. *Votes for Women: American Suffragists and the Battle for the Ballot.* Chapel Hill, NC: Algonquin Young Readers, 2018.

Dilbeck, D. H. *Frederick Douglass: America's Prophet.* Chapel Hill: University of North Carolina Press, 2018.

Ferris, Jeri Chase. *Demanding Justice: A Story about Mary Ann Shadd Cary.* Minneapolis, MN: Carolrhoda Books, 2003.

Foner, Philip S. *Frederick Douglass on Women's Rights.* New York: Da Capo Press, 1992.

Foner, Philip S., and Robert J. Branham, eds., *Lift Every Voice: African American Oratory, 1787–1900.* Tuscaloosa: University of Alabama Press, 1997.

Fradin, Dennis Brindell, and Judith Bloom Fradin. *Fight On! Mary Church Terrell's Battle for Integration.* New York: Clarion Books, 2003.

Franzen, Trisha. *Anna Howard Shaw: The Work of Woman Suffrage*. Urbana: University of Illinois Press, 2014.

Gabriel, Mary. *Notorious Victoria: The Life of Victoria Woodhull, Uncensored*. Chapel Hill, NC: Algonquin Books, 1998.

Gage, Matilda Joslyn. *Woman, Church and State: A Historical Account of the Status of Woman through the Christian Ages: With Reminiscences of the Matriarchate*. New York: The Truth Seeker Company, 1893.

Giddings, Paula J. *Ida: A Sword Among Lions: Ida B. Wells and the Campaign Against Lynching*. New York: HarperCollins, 2009.

Ginzberg, Lori D. *Elizabeth Cady Stanton: An American Life*. New York: Hill and Wang, 2009.

Harper, Ida Husted. *The Life and Work of Susan B. Anthony*. Indianapolis, IN: The Hollenbeck Press, 1898.

Hoffert, Sylvia D. *Alva Vanderbilt Belmont: Unlikely Champion of Women's Rights*. Bloomington: Indiana University Press, 2011.

Irwin, Inez Haynes. *Up Hill with Banners Flying*. Penobscot, ME: Traversity Press, 1964.

Jackson, Tricia Williams. *Women in Black History: Stories of Courage, Faith and Resilience*. Grand Rapids, MI: Revell, 2016.

Kent, Deborah. *Elizabeth Cady Stanton: "Woman Knows the Cost of Life."* Berkeley Heights, NJ: Enslow Publishers, 2010.

Hannam, June, Katherine Holden, and Mitzi Auchterlonie. *International Encyclopedia of Women's Suffrage*. Santa Barbara, CA: ABC-CLIO, 2000.

Kamma, Anne. *If You Lived When Women Won Their Rights*. New York: Scholastic, 2006.

Kerr, Andrea Moore. *Lucy Stone: Speaking Out for Equality*. New Brunswick, NJ: Rutgers University Press, 1992.

Khan, Khizr, with Anne Quirk. *This Is Our Constitution: Discover America with a Gold Star Father*. New York: Alfred A. Knopf, 2017.

Kroeger, Brooke. *The Suffragents: How Women Used Men to Get the Vote*. Albany: State University of New York Press, 2017.

Levinson, Cynthia, and Sanford Levinson. *Fault Lines in the Constitution: The Framers, Their Fights, and the Flaws that Affect Us Today*. Atlanta, GA: Peachtree Publishers, 2017.

Lunardini, Christine A. *From Equal Suffrage to Equal Rights: Alice Paul and the National Woman's Party, 1910–1928*. New York: New York University Press, 1986.

McMillan, Sally G. *Lucy Stone: An Unapologetic Life*. New York: Oxford University Press, 2015.

Million, Joelle. *Woman's Voice, Woman's Place: Lucy Stone and the Birth of the Woman's Rights Movement*. Westport, CT: Praeger Publishers, 2003.

Neuman, Johanna. *Gilded Suffragists: The New York Socialites Who Fought for Women's Right to Vote*. New York: Washington Mews Books, 2017.

Otero-Warren, Nina. *Old Spain in Our Southwest*. Chicago: Rio Grande Press, 1962.

Pankhurst, Emmeline. *My Own Story*. London: Eveleigh Nash, 1914.

Peck, Mary Gray. *Carrie Chapman Catt: A Biography.* New York: H.W. Wilson, 1944.

Pollack, Pam, and Meg Belviso. *Who Was Susan B. Anthony?* New York: Grosset & Dunlap, 2014.

Rhodes, Jane. *Mary Ann Shadd Cary: The Black Press and Protest in the Nineteenth Century.* Bloomington: Indiana University Press, 1998.

Richards, Laura Elizabeth, Maud Howe Elliott, and Florence Howe Hall. *Julia Ward Howe: 1819–1910.* Boston: Houghton Mifflin, 1915.

Ritchie, Donald A., and JusticeLearning.org. *Our Constitution.* New York: Oxford University Press, 2006.

Robertson, Stacy M. *Parker Pillsbury: Radical Abolitionist, Male Feminist.* Ithaca, NY: Cornell University Press, 2000.

Ruiz, Vicki L., and Virginia Sánchez Korrol. *Latina Legacies: Identity, Biography, and Community.* New York: Oxford University Press, 2005.

Shaw, Anna Howard, D.D., M.D., with Elizabeth Jordan. *The Story of a Pioneer.* New York: Harper & Bros., 1915.

Smith, Norma. *Jeannette Rankin: America's Conscience.* Helena: Montana Historical Society Press, 2002.

Stanton, Elizabeth Cady. *Eighty Years and More: Reminiscences 1815–1897.* New York: European Publishing, 1898.

Stauffer, John, and Henry Louis Gates Jr., eds. *The Portable Frederick Douglass.* New York: Penguin Books, 2016.

Sterling, Dorothy. *Ahead of Her Time: Abby Kelley and the Politics of Antislavery.* New York: W. W. Norton, 1991.

Stern, Phillip, ed. *The Life and Writings of Abraham Lincoln.* New York: Modern Library, 1942.

Stevens, Doris. *Jailed for Freedom: American Women Win the Vote.* Edited by Carol O'Hare. Troutdale, OR: NewSage Press, 1995.

Stone, Tanya Lee. *Elizabeth Leads the Way: Elizabeth Cady Stanton and the Right to Vote.* New York: Henry Holt, 2008.

Tartakovsky, Joseph. *The Lives of the Constitution: Ten Exceptional Minds that Shaped America's Supreme Law.* New York: Encounter Books, 2018.

Terrell, Mary Church. *A Colored Woman in a White World.* New York: G. K. Hall, 1996.

Truth, Sojourner. *Narrative of Sojourner Truth.* Boston: J. B. Yerrinton and Son, 1850.

Van Voris, Jacqueline. *Carrie Chapman Catt: A Public Life.* New York: The Feminist Press at The City University of New York, 1987.

Wagner, Sally Roesch. *Sisters in the Spirit: Haudenosaunee (Iroquois) Influence on Early American Feminists.* Summertown, TN: Native Voices, 2001.

Waldman, Michael. *The Fight to Vote.* New York: Simon & Schuster, 2016.

Walton, Mary. *A Woman's Crusade: Alice Paul and the Battle for the Ballot.* New York: Palgrave Macmillan, 2010.

Ward, Geoffrey C., Ken Burns, and Paul Barnes. *Not for Ourselves Alone: The Story of Elizabeth Cady Stanton and Susan B. Anthony*. New York: Alfred A. Knopf, 1999.

Weiss, Elaine. *The Woman's Hour: The Great Fight to Win the Vote*. New York: Viking, 2018.

Wells, Ida B. *Crusade for Justice: The Autobiography of Ida B. Wells*. Edited by Alfreda M. Duster. Chicago: University of Chicago Press, 1970.

Whaley, Charlotte. *Nina Otero-Warren of Santa Fe*. Albuquerque: University of New Mexico Press, 1994.

Whalin, W. Terry. *Sojourner Truth: American Abolitionist*. Uhrichsville, OH: Barbour Publishing, 2013.

Wheeler, Marjorie Spruill. *One Woman, One Vote: Rediscovering the Woman Suffrage Movement*. Troutdale, OR: NewSage Press, 1995.

White, Barbara A. *The Beecher Sisters*. New Haven, CT: Yale University Press, 2003.

Willard, Frances. *Glimpses of Fifty Years: The Autobiography of an American Woman*. Chicago: H. J. Smith and the Woman's Temperance Publication Association, 1889.

Woelfle, Gretchen. *Jeannette Rankin, Political Pioneer*. Honesdale, PA: Calkins Creek, 2007.

Ziegler, Valarie H. *Diva Julia: The Public Romance and Private Agony of Julia Ward Howe*. Harrisburg, PA: Trinity Press International, 2003.

Zimet, Susan. *Roses and Radicals: The Epic Story of How American Women Won the Right to Vote*. New York: Viking Books for Young Readers, 2018.

PHOTO CREDITS

INDEX

ABOUT THE AUTHOR

Author photograph by Y.E.C. Creations Photography

NANCY B. KENNEDY is a journalist and the author of seven previous books. She was born in Rochester, New York, the home of suffragist Susan B. Anthony and an epicenter of reform activity. "The suffrage fight is long and complex—but focusing on the people involved brings this intricate story to life," she says. "It is a privilege to take part in the centennial celebration of this historic victory." She lives in New Jersey with her family.